a cat abroad

Books by Peter Gethers

FICTION
The Dandy
Getting Blue

NONFICTION
Rotisserie League Baseball (coauthor)
The Cat Who Went to Paris
A Cat Abroad

a cat abroad

THE FURTHER ADVENTURES OF NORTON, THE CAT WHO WENT TO PARIS, AND HIS HUMAN

peter Gethers

CROWN PUBLISHERS, INC.   NEW YORK

Published by Crown Publishers, Inc., 201 East 50th Street, New York, New York 10022. Member of the Crown Publishing Group.

Random House, Inc. New York, Toronto, London, Sydney, Auckland

CROWN is a trademark of Crown Publishers, Inc.

Book design by June Bennett-Tantillo

Illustrations by Mary Lynn Blasutta

Manufactured in the United States of America

Library of Congress Cataloging-in-Publication Data
Gethers, Peter.
    A cat abroad: the further adventures of Norton, the cat who went to Paris, and his human / by Peter Gethers.
    1. Americans—Travel—France—Provence—Fiction.
2. Cats—Travel—France—Provence—Fiction. 3. Provence (France)—Fiction.
I. Title.
PS3557.E84C37 1993
813'.54—dc20   93-19267
                                                              CIP

ISBN 0-517-59110-3

10 9 8 7 6 5 4 3 2 1

First Edition

*To Danie, Anne, Sylvie, Jean-Guy, Anette,
Philippe, Elisabeth, Gwen, Ailie, Jenny, Jim,
Maureen, Margit, Georges, Mike, and
Deborah, who welcomed us, taught us, fed us,
and became friends forever.*

contents

acknowledgments

Leona Nevler and Betty Prashker believed, encouraged, and fixed.

Esther Newberg did her usual tooth-and-nail job and continues to be the perfect agent.

Janis seems not to care (well, sort of), no matter how grumpy I get or how many weekends I work.

And I especially want to thank Norton for letting me share the chair at my desk with him. For the next book, I hope I get a full half, but I won't count on it.

foreword

Recently, I was in Paris with my rather astonishing and extremely handsome Scottish Fold cat, Norton. We were having dinner with Danielle, an old friend of mine who lives in the 17th arrondissement, and her daughter, Priscilla. I met Priscilla when she was four years old and the only English sentence she knew was, "I like ze Beeg Mac 'amburgair." By the night of our dinner, Priscilla was no longer four. She was twenty-three, spoke fluent English, and wanted to take us to a restaurant where her boyfriend worked. Which means I'm getting longer in the tooth (not to mention thicker around the middle).

I say "we" and "us," by the way, because no one was all that excited just to see *me*. Norton was the star attraction. Danielle had made it quite clear that they would certainly be happy if I came along, but they were *really* interested in my little gray pal as their primary dinner companion. Danielle even let me know that the owner of the restaurant,

1

when told about Norton and his adventures traveling the globe, had insisted that *le chat* come to dinner as her very special guest.

When we arrived at the restaurant, Bistro d'Albert, a charming and perfect place that could exist only in France, Norton was greeted the way I imagine Ike was when he arrived at the Champs-Elysées immediately following D-Day. He was given, as he always is, his own chair, which he settled into quite comfortably. The owner, a typical somewhere-over-forty-year-old blond Frenchwoman for whom you'd happily give up the rest of your life if she'd only so much as smile at you, smiled up a storm. But not at me. Oh, no. At my innocent-looking furry friend, who, just to annoy me, I'm sure, purred like a motorboat, rolled over on his back, and practically begged the owner and all of her gorgeous waitresses to come over and scratch his stomach, which, of course, they did. Meanwhile, I was doing my best to order a *kir,* but I couldn't get anyone to even look at me.

Eventually, the waitresses returned to their regular duties, went about their work, and dinner settled into a normal routine. The three humans had a delicious bottle of red wine with their kidneys—the specialty of the house—and the cat worked away on some broiled chicken and a small bowl of milk.

One of the most satisfying things about being in Europe is that animals are treated with enormous respect. You can go into the very best, most expensive restaurants in Paris and it is almost guaranteed that someone will have brought his or her dog along for the meal. No one bats an eye, no one thinks it odd. The general feeling is that a dog has as much right to eat at Robuchon as any human. This night,

at Bistro d'Albert, *five* people brought their dogs along.
Which meant that at some point—I think it was during the
cheese course—Norton looked up from his *lait froid* to find
five curious canines of varying sizes and temperaments sitting in a circle around his chair. One of them growled.
Another worked up his courage, stuck his nose right in
Norton's face, and took a particularly antagonistic sniff. The
dogs seemed to be of the opinion that Parisian restaurants
were *their* domain and that cats should stay where they
belonged—curled up by the fireplace in a turn-of-the-
century apartment or prowling around a garden searching
for tasty mice. Certainly they did *not* belong in places where
they could actually compete for affection, much less the
boeuf bourguignon. For just a moment, the room froze. I
didn't know if French people had ever heard of the Gun-
fight at the O.K. Corral—but I had a feeling they were
about to. Except that Norton, in the peacekeeping role of
Wyatt Earp, simply looked determinedly at his ring of potential tormentors, stared each of them, one by one, straight
in the eye, then calmly went back to eating his chicken and
sipping his milk. When one dog barked, demanding a little
more attention, Norton finished chewing his last piece of
chicken, then glanced at the barker with pity, as if to say,
"Please. This is France. You're embarrassing me. Haven't
you read your Sartre?"

That was the end of the confrontation. Deflated, the dogs
went back to their respective masters and sat under their
own tables, hoping to receive a morsel of food now that
their bluff had been called.

The rest of the dinner went fairly smoothly until it came
time for dessert. Danielle, Priscilla, and I ordered our
mousse and our pastries, and when we were served, the chef

emerged from the kitchen with a big bowl of ice cream. Priscilla had mentioned to him that Norton was an ice cream fiend.

"Zees is for ze incredible cat," he told me. "I made *chocolat*—his favoreet."

Now, Norton likes his chocolate ice cream, no question about it. But he's also quite particular. He loves Ben & Jerry's. Häagen-Dazs gets an A-plus. He will eat frozen yogurt and ice milk but only in an emergency. If offered some chocolate *non*-fat frozen yogurt, he will turn his back disgustedly after one lick, making you feel as if you'd just offered a Sabrettes chili dog to the Queen of England.

The chef dug a spoon into his ice cream and held it up toward Norton. The cat eagerly took a lick, hesitated, gave some thought to what he'd just eaten—and disdainfully turned his back on the chef. I immediately had visions of the chef pulling out a glove, slapping me, and challenging me to a duel—and I was not so far off.

"It's not posseeble," he told me, totally bewildered. "Our ice cream is superb!"

"I'm sure it is," I agreed. "He's probably just full."

"But Priscilla told me he *loves* ze ice cream."

"Why don't you try giving him another taste," I suggested, although I knew my cat well enough to know this would be a useless gesture. By this time, the owner had come to the table to see what the problem was. When I explained, I could see the existential pain in her eyes.

"We have never 'ad a complaint in all our years," she told me. "Zis is outrageous."

"Give him another taste," a waitress urged.

So the chef held out a second spoonful of the stuff. Norton licked cautiously, looked at the brown lump, and, if cats can shake their heads—and I am one hundred percent cer-

tain that mine can—he shook his head. *No way,* is basically
what he was saying.

Thus ended the meal. The chef stalked back into the
kitchen, offended and insulted. The owner made it chill-
ingly clear that the cat was not nearly as special as she had
been led to believe. And I was fairly certain that the next
time the Larousse French/English Dictionary put in the
phrase "ugly American," my photo would be next to the
definition.

I gathered Norton in my arms, tried to figure out how I
could explain to a cat about the concepts of tact and eating
to be polite, gave up, and stuck him back in his cloth shoulder bag, his favorite mode of transportation.

As we were going out the door, one of the waitresses
pulled me aside.

"Your leetle cat," she said. " 'E was right."

I looked at her curiously and she explained.

"Ze chef, he made a batch of ice cream and eet was not
good," she went on. "He thought he could put one over
on ze cat and get rid of it." She put her hand on the top of
Norton's head and scratched him, something that ranks in
his top three activities. "Zat is a very impressive cat," she
said. "And his taste is *soo-pairb.*"

"I never doubted it," I told her and looked at my "leetle
cat," just a bit awed. He looked back at me, dubious. "Honest," I said to him, and held my hand over my heart. "I
never doubted you for a minute."

PART ONE

a cat at home

a cat at the super bowl

It's been said—by Edmund Wilson among other scholars—that the only great subject for American writers is the rise of America in the first half of the twentieth century.

That may be true, though I would argue that there needs to be a slight revision to such a narrow way of thinking. Without going off the deep end, let's just say: A very *good* subject for American writers is the rise of the American cat in the second half of the twentieth century. Especially if the cat happens to be a brilliant, handsome, good-hearted Scottish Fold with a round head and flat, folded ears who looks more like an owl than a cat and who has traveled all over the world, having more adventures in his travels than Gulliver.

Of course, I may be a little biased here, especially since this book is a sequel to one called *The Cat Who Went to Paris,* which was all about the aforementioned cat with folded ears and his owner, who happens to have reasonably straight ears.

The cat who did indeed go to Paris is my very own cat Norton. He's also been everywhere else in France you can think of, as well as to Holland, Germany, Italy, Switzerland, and Spain. He's been to baseball's spring training in Florida, to a writers' conference in San Diego, to meetings at movie studios in L.A., and gone cross-country skiing in Vermont. As I explained in the first book, Norton takes walks with me *sans* leash and I can leave him outside almost anyplace, in any situation, and he waits patiently in the designated spot until I come to reclaim him. Those designated spots have been everywhere from hotel lobbies to friends' backyards to airport waiting rooms to the great expanse of Central Park. He has flown on the Concorde. In Europe he goes out to restaurants with me and sits in his own chair, where he behaves like someone who has just graduated from a Swiss finishing school. He is, common to the breed, extraordinarily sweet. He is also, not common to any animal I've ever met before, shockingly smart. I really do take him everywhere I go, have ludicrously long conversations with him, and I like him so much I willingly admit it borders on the demented. Very little is done in my life unless Norton approves of the doing.

Since the publication of *The Cat Who Went to Paris,* I've discovered that, as I venture out into the world, I have begun to fade more and more into the background while Norton has slowly poked his way into the limelight. This is fine with me except it means that too often I find myself being compared, one on one, to something—excuse me: some*one*—I used to foolishly regard as my pet.

Believe me, it is not always a comforting exercise to compare cats to people, particularly if the one doing the comparing happens to be a flawed human rather than a member of the near-flawless feline race. For instance: People lie. In fact, people lie all the time. Cats do not *ever* lie. People happily kill other people in the name of everything from a god to a country to an overly developed sense of annoyance when someone cuts across two lanes on a freeway without signaling. Cats will, on occasion, kill other cats but, for the most part, they are content to puff up their fur, yowl like banshees, and rip the occasional ear off—and all this is usually done for the sake of food or protecting their own territory (which may not be condonable, but it is at least rational). People are often cruel and cause great emotional damage to others, sometimes deliberately, sometimes in blissful ignorance. The worst thing a cat will do, when it comes to inflicting emotional pain, is to make it clear he wants to be left alone. This causes nothing more than a sense of relief in other well-adjusted cats and a sense of rejection in not-so-well-adjusted, much more neurotic humans. People tend to lower their standards (and almost anything else that can be lowered) if they have the opportunity to win approval from a friend, spouse, boss, or even nodding acquaintance. Cats, on the other hand, are relatively indifferent to such emotional stroking. As a result, their decisions—on matters of personal attachments, lavishing affection, and certainly on such questions as whether or not to get off the comfortable couch to join, if they'll excuse the expression, the rat race—automatically fall on a substantially higher moral and ethical plane. All in all, it is not particularly difficult to make the case that cats are, in almost any and all ways, superior creatures to the supposedly dominant Homo sapiens.

That is why, when it came to making the single most important decision of my life—which I did last year—it is not so surprising that that decision revolved around the actions of my moral, ethical, truth-telling, affection-lavishing, semi-couch-potatoish best friend.

To begin to explain, we need to take a look at one area where people seem to hold their own, or at least can compete on the same field, with cats: courage.

Norton, not unlike most humans I have encountered, is an interesting combination of brave adventurer and wimpy coward. Plop my cat in a strange garden, yard, or even forest and he will immediately roar into action, fearlessly climbing trees, playfully slithering under bushes, joyously romping and running wherever his little gray legs will carry him. Put him down in a strange house or hotel room, and he will explore any and all nooks and crannies, generally making himself quite at home without any thought of potential danger—i.e., irate cleaning women, dizzying heights, or wobbly furniture that might not take kindly to an extra nine pounds of fur bouncing around on top of it. He is not afraid of Parisian rooftops or dark and mysterious ruins or airplanes or boats or even most dogs.

However. Two years ago, I replaced the pillows on my bed with nice, soft, down-filled ones. The night they arrived, Norton jumped up on the bed, ready for sleep, got set to nestle into his usual spot by my head, placed one tentative paw on the new pillow, and, to put it graciously, was off the bed so fast, running away from the terrifying pillow at such breakneck speed, that he made Lou Costello in *Abbott and Costello Meet Frankenstein*—and I'm talking the scene with the revolving bookshelves—look like Schwarzenegger in *T2.* It took him six months before he'd so much as *touch* a down pillow again! (Don't worry. For those of you who are already doubting my devotion, yes, I did put the old pillows back on the bed. I kept both sets handy at all times and arranged them so I could sleep on the new ones and Norton could sleep on the old ones.)

Janis—of whom much was spoken in the first book and of whom much more will be spoken in this sequel—and I recently bought a new couch for our Sag Harbor house. Only after the old couch was carried out and far removed from sight would Norton so much as step one gray and black ringed foot into the den. He had an absolute horror of that couch. He was too afraid even to *scratch* it. For those of you who are already wondering to what lengths I'll go to keep my cat happy, no, I *didn't* buy a new couch because Norton hated the old one. We got a new one because the old one was ugly, falling apart, and extremely uncomfortable. The fact that I let my cat live with something he didn't like is, however, totally out of character. In retrospect, I'm already feeling guilty and I just hope he settles in happily on the armrest of the new sofa or I'm sure I'll be furniture shopping before very long.

Janis also just bought a new blanket for our bed. A plain, simple, ordinary, purple, inanimate, wool blanket. There is nothing remotely threatening about this blanket—except to a particular Scottish Fold. To Norton, this blanket has much the same personality as Freddy Krueger in *Nightmare on Elm Street*. The first time Janis picked him up, put him on the bed, and, thus, on the dreaded blanket, Norton did a near-perfect Greg Louganis back flip onto the floor—I gave him a 9.7—and disappeared from sight for the rest of the day.

In addition to the odd piece of furniture and accompanying accoutrements, my dear cat also is terrified of bicycles, jackhammers, and birds. The first two I can sympathize with. Bicycles are ridden by careless humans and are more than capable of squashing a feline flat as a stepped-on morsel of Pounce, Norton's personal favorite between-meal snack.

And jackhammers are loud, earth-moving things and *should* be terrifying to anyone with any sense who's not named Rocco or Deke. The last one on the list, however, is a constant source of humiliation to all who know and love cat and cat owner.

This past autumn, while my round-headed pal and I were spending time in the south of France, I decided to show off *l'intelligence incroyable de mon chat.* We were going out to dinner with a friend and our car was parked several streets away from the house. I decided I'd bring Norton along to dinner—and I also decided I'd let him walk to the car with us. Our friend was a little dubious, especially because the town we were in was a French medieval mountain specialty with winding narrow streets and animals roaming freely wherever they chose to roam. But Norton came through with flying colors: striding boldly out the door, disdainfully ignoring all the dogs and cats frolicking around him, as well as all the kids kicking a soccer ball to and fro and all the adults briskly strolling around with their baguettes tucked under their arms. He followed at an acceptable pace along the cobblestones—until we came to a house, a mere ten feet away from our car, that had a bird cage hanging outside the window. Inside the cage were three tiny yellow birds, whistling and singing away. Norton, having braved all the tough obstacles in town, got within a foot of the cage, heard the birds merrily chirping, turned on his heels, and made a beeline for home, in the process breaking A. J. Foyt's land-speed record by a comfortable margin. I found him huddled pathetically by our doorway, trying his best to make himself invisible.

"They were *birds,* " I told him, shaking my head. "*Tiny* birds. *Really* tiny birds. In a *cage.* In a *locked* cage," I added, hoping to shame him.

It's very hard to argue with a cat, however, particularly a nervous cat, and clearly this cat had no intention of getting close to those tiny, caged birds again if he could help it. Which he could. So I picked him up and carried him all the way back to the car. When we passed those tiny little birds, Norton buried his head under my arm, doing his very best ostrich impersonation. Once we reached the safety of our red Citroën, he settled happily onto the backseat, and then, oblivious to the scorn with which he was greeted from his dinner companions, thoroughly enjoyed the rest of his evening on the town. There were no birds in the restaurant to disturb his meal.

While *les oiseaux* seem to be somewhat of an Achilles heel, Norton has a very wide macho streak as far as mice are concerned. This predatory instinct came as something of a shock to me when it finally surfaced. Norton and I had spent many years together without his ever exhibiting one iota of lionlike interest in chasing after big game. Then, one night, while I still had a summer house in the town of Fair Harbor, on Fire Island, the hunter was unleashed.

I was bacheloring it up this particular Saturday night with my friend Norm, the head writer of "Sesame Street" and, as chronicled in *The Cat Who Went to Paris,* legendary lady-killer of the Fair Harbor "sixishes." With us was my cousin Jon, an actor visiting from L.A. The three of us—the *four* of us, counting you-know-who—were having dinner, male-bonding, and basically having a terrific time, all the while wondering how soon we could ditch the other guys and go out and try to find a woman. As we were talking, I noticed that Jon had a big smile on his face and that he was focused on something a few feet from the dinner table.

"What are you looking at?" I wanted to know.

"Nothing," he said. "I'm just enjoying watching Norton play with his mouse toy."

I nodded, smiling at the thought and listening to Norton thrash around on the floor. And then the smile faded. Norm and I looked at each other, confused, and we both said, at the exact same time: "Norton doesn't *have* a mouse toy."

The ensuing action really should have been captured as an Impressionist painting with the title "Three Jews in the Country" because you haven't seen three fairly creaky guys move so quickly in your entire life. Jon, I believe, was standing on his chair. I'm pretty sure that I was all the way up on the table, saying something constructive like "Oh my god, I'm going to be sick!" Norm was the only one with the presence of mind to move for the broom. Using the straw end, he managed to maneuver the thrashing mouse away from Norton, who was playfully batting it around as if the room were one large knock-hockey board game. Clearly my cat did not realize that the small gray thing moving at the speed of light was a disgusting rodent to be feared and avoided at all costs. He didn't even think it was something to kill and eat for dessert. No, judging from this first close encounter of the mouse kind, Norton thought the squeaking, long-tailed prey was something to have fun with, not all that different from a catnip-stuffed beanbag.

Unfortunately for my dignity and sense of self-respect, at some point I had to climb down off the table and hold the door open while Norm swatted the mouse outside, *way* too close to my bare feet, which I pointed out to him later.

Once the creature was out of the house, we settled down and sanity reigned again. We all applauded Norton for his ability to spontaneously tap into his savage jungle instincts, and we all decided that perhaps city life was better for us humans than this dangerous living close to the ocean. More than anything, the three of us were happy we'd all struck out that weekend so that no one of the opposite sex had seen our rather tragic failure when confronted face to face with the wilds of nature. (In later retellings, the mouse became more of a rat—sometimes something closer to a small alligator—and I was the one with the broom, but I'm afraid Norm might read this, so I'd better stick to the sad truth.)

That was only the beginning, however, for Norton, so to speak, had tasted blood.

Fire Island was behind us, the charming country house in Sag Harbor was now before us, and I no longer had to worry about being humiliated in front of strange women because Janis was now a major part of the equation. I could simply worry about being humiliated in front of my very own girlfriend.

Not long after buying our house, I padded downstairs on a perfect autumn morn, went to the market to buy the papers, made a steaming pot of coffee, carried a mug of java into the safe, warm confines of the den, glanced down at the floor . . . and found a half-eaten, dead-as-a-doorknob mouse waiting for me in the middle of the room.

My very own cat had done this. The cat whom I often (probably too often) kissed right smack dab on the lips. The cat who was quite probably the sweetest, gentlest animal in existence. My genius, world-traveling cat had bitten a mouse right in half and left him as a little present for his dad.

I have to admit that, once I got over my immediate sense of revulsion, my chest puffed out a bit with pride. Okay, so birds were scary—but no three-inch-long cheese eater could push *my* cat around.

The only problem left to solve was how to actually dis-

pose of the body. Norton, by this time, was hovering outside the den, waiting for praise for his newfound role as
protector of the household. I indulged him in this, picking
him up and petting him profusely, marveling at his courage and physical prowess. Unfortunately, Janis was also
hovering around, demanding that I get rid of the corpse
immediately.

You may have picked up on the fact that I'm a tad squea-
mish when it comes to things like dead mice (for the record,
also when it comes to live snakes and any bugs larger than
a quarter). But, since my cat had moved up to a new level
of macho-hood, I was determined to do the same. And
despite what Janis would tell you now if you could talk to
her directly, I did a very solid and impressive job of mouse
removal. It just took me a while, that's all. Like about two
hours, because every time I worked up the nerve to try to
scoop the repulsive little pile onto the dustpan, I'd get dizzy
and go into the kitchen (where Janis, I might add, was safely
sequestered!) and take half an hour to get myself back
together.

After that first kill, however, the routine got a little easier
for all of us. I don't want anyone to get the impression that
our house is a mini-version of *Willard* and that thousands
of mice roam around freely, rearranging the furniture and
making crank phone calls in the middle of the night, but
once or twice a year we do have a little critter who decides
to explore under the sink or behind the refrigerator. And
once or twice a year, Norton goes into action. For a cat
whose favorite hobby, as he gets a little older, is to sit
absolutely motionless for as long as possible, it is a wonder
to behold when Norton's mouse antenna goes up. He will
sit, poised to strike, staring at a crack under the fridge, as
lithe and graceful as any tai chi master. Suddenly, an object

will dart out, so fast it's almost impossible to see, except Norton will not only see him, he'll dart even faster. And before you know it, a victorious Norton will be parading into the living room with a conquered mouse firmly clenched between his teeth. One small step for felinehood, one giant step for a mouse-free home.

I can deal with this sort of disruption much better now. Practice does indeed make perfect. No longer do I freeze at the thought of placing another body into the mouse morgue. No longer does some late, lamented Mickey Doe have to sit in the middle of the floor for hours while I stop my stomach from doing flip-flops. Nope. Now I've got things under control. Either I call my friend David Meves, who lives a couple of blocks away and, as near as I can tell, has no fear of man *or* mouse, or I have David's wife, Peggy, do it.

But I don't discuss Norton's heroics just to show off the fact that, when push comes to shove, my little cat can hold his own in time of macho crisis. I don't want him to turn into a feline Mike Tyson or Stormin' Norman Schwarzkopf. I bring it up because Norton's sense of adventure and general fearlessness had a somewhat larger effect on me and my life than simply getting me to toss out my mousetraps. Last year, I was faced with the major, life-changing decision I hinted about earlier and, as with all life-changing decisions I'd made over the past eight years, Norton was a crucial and essential part of the process.

This particular process began when I was invited to go to the Super Bowl.

I'm your basic sports fanatic, although much less so as I've gotten older, as athletes have gotten greedier, and team owners have gotten stupider. I've been to World Series games and NBA All-Star games and French Open tennis matches, but I'd never been to a Super Bowl, much less a Super Bowl in which my beloved Giants were playing. The thought of seeing L.T. leaping tall AFCers in a single bound was too good an opportunity to pass up, especially since the people who'd done the inviting were the NFL, which meant seeing him leap from fifty-yard-line seats.

Even Janis, who would normally prefer something pleasant and relaxing—like walking across hot coals or discussing the right-to-life issue with Rush Limbaugh—to attending a sports event, decided she couldn't pass up a Super Bowl. So we made our arrangements. A flight into Tampa. A room at the Dolphin Hotel in Orlando. Dinner with a honcho from NFL Properties. A cat who was a big Giants fan.

Norton had, by this time in his life, traveled extensively all over Europe and America. But even for him, Super Bowl weekend was something extraordinary.

First of all, the Dolphin Hotel is part of Disney World. As we were checking in, we were greeted by a bevy of very friendly six-foot-high, three-fingered mice dancing and prancing around the lobby, waving at anyone who'd look at them. For a human being, this is a rather disorienting sight; I can't *imagine* what could have been running through the brain of a reasonably sophisticated Scottish Fold. The prospect of biting one of these suckers in half and leaving him in the den for Dad to clean up must have been incredibly intimidating. Luckily, as I signed us into our room, Norton restrained himself admirably and settled for sticking his head out of his shoulder bag and swiveling his neck in every which direction, awestruck as he peered around the lobby.

When we went out for a stroll to take in the sights—

neither Janis nor Norton had ever been to Orlando before—the atmosphere was no less circuslike. Not only did my cat get a look at thousands of people from all over the country, drinking up a storm and determined to have as wild a weekend as possible, he saw screaming vendors hawking T-shirts and team sweat suits, screaming kids dragging their screaming parents across the street to Disney World, and screaming NFL marketing men trying to stop everybody else from screaming so they could scream louder about their thrice-too-expensive wares. In addition to the giant mice, Norton also got a very good gander at Goofy and Donald, up close and personal, as well as all the real-life (and sculptures of) fish, which were everywhere you looked in the hotel (the designers obviously felt a compunction to create an artistic theme worthy of the hotel's name).

After two days of hectic touristing and socializing, Norton, Janis, and I had a quiet few moments in our room before we were to join all the screaming people on the bus that was to take us to the game.

"Are you glad you came?" I asked Janis, figuring that with only the upcoming game left on our weekend agenda, it would all be downhill from here.

"Sort of," she grudgingly said. "Although I still say it was Goofy who pinched me at that party last night."

"How about you?" I said to my cat. In response, Norton sprawled out on the bed and turned over on his back, his subtle way of telling me he was both tired and wanted his belly scratched.

"What must it be like for him?" I asked Janis. "Giant mice. Lunatic football fans. Kids with buffaloes painted on their chests. For us this is just a weird and fun weekend. For Norton, this must be like going to *Mars*."

As we talked, I started to obsess more and more about the level of high adventure Norton had reached that weekend. Sure, he'd enjoyed the café life in Paris, liked sunning himself on Florida beaches, even got used to cross-country skiing in Vermont. But this weekend, this was something he'd never come close to seeing or doing before.

"For *real*," I said, half to Janis, half to myself. "I'm kind of jealous. *Nothing* we do could possibly be as strange and exciting and out of the ordinary as what this cat's doing."

Janis knows enough not to encourage me when I start trying to delve into the mind of my cat (or my own mind, for that matter). So she kept quiet and let me go on.

"It's depressing, is what it is," I began to rant. "We're people, he's a cat! We can't let him lead a better life than we're leading!"

"He leads a better life than anyone else in the whole *world* is leading," Janis pointed out.

"That's beside the point," I came back with. "He deserves it. And I'm not talking about Norton in particular. I'm talking philosophically."

Resigned now, Janis sighed and asked me what I was really getting at.

"Norton's life is exciting. He hunts. He prowls. He goes to Mars. Our life is dull. We go to work, we watch TV. We're stuck in a routine. I want my life to be as adventurous as my cat's!"

"Okay," Janis said, doing her best to humor me. "What exactly do you want to do about it?"

To her credit, when I told her, she didn't gasp, shriek, or faint. What she did was ask me if I was serious, and when I said I was, she said, "Okay."

I decided I wanted us to do something as adventurous as Norton coming to the Mars Super Bowl. So we did.

Which is how I came to quit my very good job, leave my very nice apartment, pack up my entire very nice life, and, with my very understanding girlfriend and my role model of a cat, move to the south of France.

a cat lost

It was not as easy as all that, of course. There were minor odds and ends and major life changes to take care of before the three of us could charge ahead to new glory in the old world.

The first thing we had to consider were our jobs. Janis, who had worked since she was fourteen years old and was something of a workaholic (and a very successful workaholic), arranged for a year's sabbatical from her job in publishing. With that load off her shoulders, she began worrying about a new load: What the hell would she actually *do* for a whole year?

I, as usual, was worried about having *too* much to do. I took care of part of that by resigning as publisher of the company I ran. The chairman of the board I resigned to was quite understanding.

"I no longer get to do what I like," I told him. "All I

do now is talk to lawyers and try to solve other people's problems."

"How do you think *I* feel?" was his response.

I saw his point but I held fast, and he proved he was a good chairman by solving my problem and giving me the perfect job, letting me throw off all the bad parts of what I was doing—the bureaucratic tanglings and business hassles—and go back to what I liked to do, which was working with authors and trying to be creative. And, once he got over the shock, he even agreed to let me do it from France.

The next thing to do was break it to my California agent that my TV and movie career—such as it was—was going to be put on hold for a year. He took the news surprisingly well, which made me think that my TV and movie career probably was *already* on hold. This did not particularly sadden me.

One of the reasons I was able to pack it all in for a while was that my partner, David Handler, and I had been hired to write and produce a TV series that year. It had started out with great promise: a decent premise for the show, a pleasant enough staff of writers, and a terrific cast, TV stars who were actually good actors. The first day the writing staff got together, David and I had visions of a Cosby-like syndication check one day making its way into our dwindling bank accounts.

As is usually the case when one gets one's hopes up in show business, it was not to be.

One of the most amazing things about the television business is the way people delude themselves (which is probably why those delusionless creatures, cats, have never made their mark in TV). People who create shows like "My Mother the Car" and "Pink Lady and Jeff" can't live with

themselves if they actually face up to what they're promul-
gating on society, so they convince themselves that they're
really doing Neil Simon. People who do the *good* stuff on
TV—shows like "Cheers" and "Taxi" and "Hill Street
Blues"—start to think they're Arthur Miller. There's a famous story about a well-known TV producer who had just
produced one of the great disasters of a particular season.
Not only was the show ridiculed for its shockingly low
quality, it was canceled after one episode (which is the only
thing people in TV are *really* sensitive to being ridiculed
about). After the cancellation notice came, the producer
started ranting and raving to his partner. "The problem
was, we were ahead of our time," he insisted. "The show
was too good! The American public wasn't ready for it!"
His partner let him carry on for as long as he could stand
it, then finally interrupted with these immortal words of a
rare television realist: "You know, you're right," he said.
"We *were* ahead of our time. The American public just
wasn't ready for total shit."

Needless to say, the partnership broke up.

Unfortunately for us, however, we had one of those I'm-
a-Genius mentalities running the show David and I had
signed on for. He opened one of our first story conferences
by telling us he thought that a good sitcom script was as
good as the best poetry. Great. He didn't just think he was
Neil Simon or Arthur Miller. We had a producer/director
who thought he was W. B. Yeats. Maybe we could do a
show called "I Love Leda and the Swan" or a "Gilligan's
Island Sails to Byzantium" reunion special.

We knew we were in trouble when, during the course of
writing the first thirteen episodes and shaping the show,
people all around us started to get fired. The co-executive
producer was the first to go. Then a couple of writers fell

by the wayside (including one who, after we'd had a discussion about a zany episode that would center around a botched surprise party, said, "This show has the potential to be so Chekhovian"). New writers were hired and then they, too, were fired (one was hired to be a consultant, came in for one meeting, argued with the boss, and was immediately fired. Actually, not so immediately that he wasn't given a large check to keep him happy. This made the other writers, who were working hard but weren't getting large checks, somewhat cranky). Then, as if things weren't bad enough, we got a close-up gander at the female star, who was, according to the premise of the show, supposed to be gorgeous, sexy, and irresistible. Unfortunately, the only person she could have possibly been irresistible to would have been Dumbo because our star had gained a good thirty pounds since her glory days.

Things went downhill from there. But we knew we were in *serious* trouble after we saw what happened to our first script. David and I tend to take the realistic approach. We were aware we weren't on the Preston Sturges level with our contributions to the show, but we were confident that our forty-four-page work was extremely funny. And while it may not have been Yeats (or even Ogden Nash), it was, we knew, coherent. However, when we were given a cassette to watch after the filming and editing, we were a tad surprised to find that not only were all our jokes cut out, the show made no sense. None. I'm talking total gibberish. Our nemesis had managed to rewrite it and then cut it so any stranger watching it would have absolutely no idea what it was about. Plus, what was supposed to be a lighthearted contemporary comedy now had all the wit and style of one of Eva Braun's home movies. To top it all off, *our* names were plastered all over the credits.

Here's how bad it was: Norton, who liked hanging around the set, had, midway through our viewing of the show's first act, gone and hid in the office's heating duct. He decided that crawling around in old, rusty pipes was a lot more fun than watching his dad's career die a slow and painful death.

As soon as the tape finished rolling, the door to our office was thrown open and it was the producer/director, the man responsible for this entire nightmare.

"I think it's the most brilliant thing I've ever done," he announced.

We said nothing.

"I think it may be the greatest show in the history of television," he now proclaimed. I'm not kidding. He really said that.

We still said nothing. If ever the phrase "Silence is golden" had meaning, this was the time, but we knew that at some point we'd have to work up our courage and speak. The psycho in our office decided there was no time like the present.

"Didn't *you* think it was *great?*" he demanded.

"Well," we both hemmed and hawed, "we thought it was very good. But we think there might be room for improvement. Maybe we can give you a few notes."

"I don't *take* notes on something that's *perfect!*" he told us. He didn't actually say the words "you barbarian ignoramuses" out loud, but his tone made it quite clear that the phrase should have been tacked on to the end of his sentence. Then he slammed the door on his way out, leaving us to realize that we were working for a lunatic and we could forget about making enough money from this series to buy a small, private island in the Caribbean.

David and I lasted for three more painful months before

our greed finally gave way to our self-respect and we quit. The only satisfying thing was that the show folded immediately after we did.

I had learned a couple of valuable lessons, though, which I promise never to forget. One is that I will never again work with people who don't believe that something they do can ever be improved upon in some way, shape, or form. That attitude is the antithesis of all creativity. The second thing I learned is that I will never again doubt my cat's taste. The next time he walks out of a show, so do I.

Free at last, I was in relatively good shape for a change of life. Janis was all set, too. Only Norton now had to be dealt with.

Two things were stopping us from leaving immediately. The first was probably the worst and scariest day of my life: the day Norton ran away and got lost in New York City.

The trauma started simply enough. Janis and I made plans to take a short trip—a trip *without* Norton. This is not something I'm usually wont to do, but my back was to the wall. Janis comes from the South, her family's still down there, she still has enough Southern lilt in her voice to sound as if she could have Stanley Kowalski as a brother-in-law, and, to top it all off, her father had a big birthday coming up—so she decided that we had to venture south of New Jersey for a week before we blew off the United States for good. We decided to fly to Memphis, then spend a week driving further down, through Mississippi to New Orleans. This was not a trip Norton could make. He could happily live with the several hours we'd spend every day in the car; I knew he wouldn't mind moving to a new hotel every night; and I was fairly sure he'd like to discover real Southern barbecue. But it simply wasn't practical. When traveling in Europe, he was used to being greeted with open arms by

both restaurants and hotels. On the road in America, however, he couldn't eat out with us and we couldn't be sure that
any of the hotels we'd find would take him. I had a crucial
decision to make. On the one hand I could leave Norton for
seven days with his usual cat-sitter, Lynn Waggoner, his
favorite nonimmediate family member in the world. On the
other hand, I could try being in the car with Janis on a rainy
night in the backwoods of Mississippi trying to explain to her
that the hotel we'd been lucky enough to find wouldn't let us
in because they didn't take cats. I decided I'd rather face
Norton's disappointment than Janis's wrath.

Naturally, I made the wrong choice.

We did nothing different to prepare for this excursion, so
don't ask me how my cat could possibly know that he wasn't
coming along on the trip—but he definitely, unequivocally,
one hundred percent, absolutely knew. A couple of days
before we were to leave, I noticed that he seemed to be
sulking. Whenever I say things like, "I think Norton's upset
because he's not coming on our trip" to Janis, she tries to
get me to see a good psychiatrist, so I usually keep such
thoughts to myself. This time was no different—I kept
quiet. But he was definitely out of sorts.

Janis was going to Memphis on a Friday. That was also
my final day in the office, the day of the big farewell party,
so I was going to stick around and meet up with her on
Saturday. I was also having dinner that night with one of the
Random House bigwigs, the nephew of the company's
owner. All in all, it seemed worth sticking around for.

We—Janis, Norton, and I—spent Thursday night at
Janis's apartment. I woke up bright and early Friday morn,
fed Norton his breakfast, then went in to take a shower.
When I came out, I got dressed, kissed my still-sleeping
girlfriend on the top of the head, and went to gather up my

cat to take him to the office. When the company told me they were going to throw me a farewell party, they made it fairly clear that they wanted the chance to say farewell to Norton as well.

I called him, waiting for him to come as usual, but there was no response. I waited patiently—still nothing. I began poking around in some of his usual resting places—but no Scottish Fold anywhere. I then spent twenty minutes looking through Janis's apartment and could find no trace of Norton. Annoyed—what a time for him to decide to act like a regular cat—I went in, woke Janis up, and told her I was going to leave Norton behind.

"He's hiding," I said. "I'm sure he'll come out as soon as I leave. Have a good flight and I'll just come back and pick him up after work. See you tomorrow."

And off I went.

At noon Janis called my office.

"I'm leaving for the airport," she told me. "Norton still hasn't come out. I don't know if he's still in the apartment."

"Of *course* he's still in the apartment," I told her, a little annoyed. "Where could he have gone?"

"I don't know," she admitted. "I can't figure out any way he could have gotten out, but I really looked for him. And I don't think he's here."

"He's just being a cat," I said confidently. "Cats hide all the time. We're just not used to *Norton* doing it. He'll be waiting for me when I come to get him."

She acknowledged that I knew my cat better than she did and went off to Memphis. I stuck around, ate some cake and drank some wine at the farewell party, then around four in the afternoon I went back to Janis's to pick up what I was sure would be a repentant Norton.

When I walked in the front door I called his name. Silence. I tried again, gently cooing for him. Zilch. For the first time since cat and I had joined our lives together, I got a nervous flutter in my stomach.

I began to *really* search the apartment.

I looked in the closets. I took things out of the closets. I stood on chairs and peered into corners of the highest bookshelves. I crawled under beds. Gently calling Norton's name every few seconds.

No cat.

Now, I am a reasonably mature person. I have had my share of traumatic experiences and emergencies and have handled them all with, I like to think, a certain amount of grace and strength. I'm not prone to overreaction, panic, or hysteria. But, at the moment I decided that my nine-pound, extremely trusting, wonderfully sweet, and extremely protected cat was outside, loose on the mean streets of New York City, I overreacted, panicked, and became completely hysterical. To make matters worse, the weather immediately turned hurricanelike: Gusts of wind, explosions of thunder, flashes of lightning, and sheets of rain took over the city. As I pictured little Norton outside in all that, I lost whatever inner fortitude I'd ever pretended to have and simply began blubbering pathetically.

The first thing I did was call my friends Kathleen and Dominick. Kathleen is one of my very closest pals and would do anything for me. Dominick speaks with a British accent, so I knew he wouldn't go emotional on me and would keep his head. Through pathetic gasps and strangled sobs, I managed to spell out the problem. Half an hour later, they were down at Janis's apartment, helping me rip the place apart.

"Norton is *definitely* here," Dominick said. "There is no question about it."

His confidence buoyed my spirits a little, but the buoy sank fairly quickly as we kept searching the place to no avail.

We moved couches. We took every single item out of Janis's closets. We lifted radiator covers and floorboards, shifted large, unbelievably heavy kitchen appliances, and called Norton's name as calmly as we could—but there was no sign of him whatsoever. That was when I spied the open window.

You must understand something: We kept the windows closed, except for a crack, whenever Norton was staying in that apartment. But as my eyes were scanning every inch of the place, desperate for any sign of feline life, I spotted a living room window that was open at most three inches—and open from the top, perhaps twelve feet off the ground. It would have been a herculean feat, involving a jump to a chair, another jump to the top of a bookshelf, then an incredibly difficult leap up to and through a three-inch-wide crack—but I was convinced that it was through that crack Norton had disappeared. No matter that the trip down would have been even more difficult—either a tough jump up to the roof and then on to who knows where or a very difficult shinny down the front of the building to the street. I was positive I'd discovered the escape route. So we went in search of the escapee.

We immediately began a tour of the Soho neighborhood, in weather that now seemed to be a full-fledged tornado.

The three of us went to every store within two blocks of the apartment and asked if they'd seen a small, gray, wet cat with folded ears. No one had seen anything except three drenched, crazy-looking people in search of a lost feline.

We then scoured every nook and cranny and back alleyway within the same two-block range, screaming out Norton's name whenever we saw a potential hiding place for a wayward cat. But no wayward cat appeared (and the only positive that came out of this exercise is that I learned Linda Winer's Cat Law #3. Linda Winer is a columnist for *Newsday* and friend of mine who, at various points in her life, has owned several dozen cats, including one named Ishkabibble. Linda's Cat Law #3 is a simple one, written in stone after Ishkabibble disappeared one day and Linda had to search high and low for him all over her neighborhood: Never Name Your Cat Something You Are Ashamed to Yell Out Loud at the Top of Your Lungs).

We split up at this point, having failed to find Norton close to home. Dominick and Kathleen broadened our horizon, moving several blocks farther away, still checking for any buildings and alleys that might look inviting, warm, and dry to a frightened cat. My assignment was to get Janis's landlady to take me into their backyard. They had a decent-sized garden and patio, with a garage/workshop. It was reasonably familiar territory, I realized. Norton might have fled there figuring I'd be able to find him eventually. I was just hoping-beyond-hope that he'd figured right.

Janis's landlady wasn't home yet, but the landlady's mother, who also lives in the building, was. She was kind enough to use her key to let me back. Unfortunately, she also decided to accompany me.

She's a terrific woman, Mrs. Flaymen, but she's also eighty years old and has a slight hearing problem—as in, she can't hear anything anyone says. It's difficult to stress exactly how upset I was; just accept the fact that I was bordering on irrational behavior. So I was not at my best for the conversation that transpired in the pouring rain, in the nooks and crannies of Mrs. Flaymen's backyard.

"Ohhhh, the poor cat," she began.

I didn't want to hear about the poor cat. I wanted to hear

that he was dry and safe. So I acknowledged her despair only with a grim nod.

"How old is he?" she wanted to know.

"Eight years old," I told her.

"Four weeks old!" she screeched. "Oh my God!"

"Eight *years*," I said again. "He's *eight!"*

"How could you let a four-week-old kitten outside?! And in weather like this!"

Normally, I would find this kind of inane miscommunication fairly funny. Perhaps even hilarious. However, in the midst of my desperate search, I had, possibly for the first time in my life, completely lost my sense of humor. So I did my best to ignore her and started looking through the garden.

"What's his name?" she asked me as I prowled.

"Norton," I muttered.

"Morris?!" she said.

"Norton!" I told her. *"Not Morris! Norton!"*

"Morris!" she began to call. "Come here, Morris!"

"Norton," I growled. "His name's Norton!"

"Morris!" she kept shouting. And then she started muttering about how stupid I was to let a one-week-old kitten outside in a hurricane.

"His name's not Morris!" I finally screamed. "His name's Norton! And he's not one week old! He's not even four weeks old! He's eight!"

"One week, four weeks, eight weeks," she said. "What's the difference?"

"Eight *years!"* I yelled as loud as I could yell. "Eight years!!!!"

"I don't think it makes a difference," she said with a shrug. "I'm sure he's dead."

I'll skip the rest of the conversation, as well as any detailed description of the veins bulging in my neck, and just say that my scrupulous search of the back of the apartment house was as fruitful as the searching I'd done up till then. There was nary a sign of my beloved cat.

I met Kathleen and Dominick back at the apartment at the appointed time. They were as wet as I was and had also had the same rotten luck. I called the number where Janis was staying in Memphis and left the following message on her friend's phone machine, in a monotone that could, putting the most positive possible spin on it, only be described as zombielike: "Hi. It's me. Still no sign. He's gone. I don't know what to do. I'm not coming tomorrow. I have to wait here until he shows up." I don't think I was even able to say good-bye. I just choked my message off in mid-sob and hung up. That was the fourth or fifth such message I'd left for her.

By this time, the entire block was involved in the search. Janis's landlady, Sylvia, had come home, heard the frantic activity, and learned what had happened. She started calling all her neighbors and pretty soon everybody was calling everybody else, seeing if anyone had seen a lost cat with strange ears. One kindly person called Janis's apartment and told me that she had definitely seen Norton. But, as I probed a bit, it turned out that she'd spotted a stray cat in her yard the day before. Sorrowfully, I explained that Norton had only gotten out that very morning, and that it was some other miserable person who'd be searching for yesterday's stray.

It was now seven-thirty at night, so in addition to the storm, it was getting quite dark. It was also time for my dinner with Mr. Random House. There was nothing I could do for Norton—not at this point—so I did my best to look presentable and went off to the restaurant. I decided I'd return to Janis's after dinner and spend the whole rest of the night waiting and/or searching.

The dinner was a disaster from start to finish. I'd be asked a question along the lines of, "Well, what kind of direction do you foresee for the company over the next few years?" and I'd come back with a morose reply along the lines of, "Huh?" Then I'd stare vacantly at the wall for five minutes, the silence being broken only by my long and loud sighs. We made it through the salad and main course and on to the dessert in a leisurely twenty minutes or so. I had no appetite and my total depression put an obvious pall on the executive's appetite. I think it also put the same pall on his opinion of me, but what could I do? As far as I was concerned, life as I knew it was over.

As we were waiting for the check to arrive, the waitress came over to our table and said to me, "Excuse me, but are you Mr. Gethers?" When I told her I was, she let me know that there was a phone call for me.

The call was from Janis and it was the most wonderful call I'd ever received in my life.

"You're not going to believe it," she began, "but go to my apartment immediately. Norton's waiting for you in the living room."

I let out a very loud yelp, tried to calm myself down since I was in public, then said the hell with it and let out another yelp, louder than the first. I pleaded with Janis to tell me how this miracle had occurred.

"I told you you're not going to believe it," she said, and then proceeded to relate the entire story: After landing at the airport and going straight out to dinner, she'd finally gotten to her friends' house in Memphis, where she found my many suicidal-sounding phone-machine messages waiting for her. Not knowing what else to do, she called her landlady and asked her to send her husband up onto the roof in one last desperate attempt to find the cat. According to the landlady, her husband's not unwarranted response was, "What are you, out of your mind?!" and her response to that was a slow, quiet, and obviously quite effective: "Get . . . out . . . on . . . the . . . fucking . . . roof. *Now*."

She then went up the two flights to Janis's apartment, figuring that if Norton was indeed up on the roof, he would be so petrified and hard to handle that her husband would need someone to hand him to, through the window. She turned the key to the front door, stepped inside . . . and sitting in the foyer, curled up in a calm, peaceful, untraumatized, toasty-warm ball, was none other than Norton the cat.

Stunned, she ran to the phone and called Janis in Memphis, who immediately called me at the restaurant. I hung up the restaurant phone, told my confused dinner partner—who'd clearly crossed my name off his list marked "People with a Future to Whom I Might Pay Lots of Money Someday"—that life was good again, then I raced back to Janis's in a cab, taking the three flights up to the apartment two stairs at a time. By the time I got there, Sylvia had put Norton in one of the apartment's two bedrooms, closing the door behind him so he couldn't possibly get out and hide again. When I inched the door open—still not believing the little guy was really there—I found Norton sound asleep on the bed in his usual position: head on the pillow, body tucked under the blanket. When I stepped inside, he opened one eye and began purring.

I gently walked over, picked him up, and began a rather lengthy petting, scratching, cooing, and kissing process. When both of us had had enough of that, I called Janis.

"He's actually here," I told her. For the first time in fourteen hours, my voice didn't have that despairing rasp to it.

"And he'd *never* been outside?" she asked, incredulous.

"Nope. He's as dry and happy as could be."

"Then where was he?" she wanted to know—the first of several million times we asked ourselves that question.

We never found out where he was. We did eventually figure out that this day-long hide-and-seek experience was Norton's little way of letting us know he didn't like being left behind for a week while his parents went off on a fun vacation (and, believe me, now Janis accepts it as gospel when I tell her that Norton's looking a little subdued—she instantly goes through her apartment, closing the door to every room). But, more immediately, as we spoke on the phone, as I did everything but collapse in relief and exhaustion, Janis got angry. In her own way, she'd been as unnerved by the experience as I'd been, and she had the same feeling, I imagine, one has when a child falls off a high swing yet doesn't hurt himself. At first you're so relieved he's okay, you'll do anything to make him happy. Then, when the scare's over, you want to kill him for putting himself—and you—through the trauma.

"Don't let him get away with this," Janis told me. "I don't think you should feed him tonight."

"You're right," I agreed, nodding vigorously. "I definitely won't feed him."

"And don't pet him and kiss him and tell him that everything's okay," she ordered.

"Absolutely not," I said. "I'd never do that. I'll be strict and firm."

"Yeah," she said dubiously.

"Yeah!" I said strictly and firmly, if a bit guiltily.

"I'll see you tomorrow," she said, unconvinced. "And I'm glad your stupid cat's okay."

"Thank you. I'll tell him."

"And don't feed him. I *mean* it. It's for his own good."

"As of now," I insisted, "he's on bread and water. Think of me as George Kennedy in *Lonely Are the Brave.*"

When I start making movie references that she doesn't get, Janis usually figures it's time to hang up. I knew, at that very moment, before the phone even clicked down into the cradle in Memphis, she was turning to her friends and telling them there was no way I wasn't going to cave in. I could tell she thought I'd be feeding and petting my cat within seconds. But I was determined to toe the line. Tough love was my new motto for the evening.

Unfortunately for my new motto, it's almost impossible to resist a meowing Scottish Fold. Especially one of his special "I'm hungry" meows.

"No dinner for you," I told him as definitively as I was able. "*You* are being punished. And that is *all* there is to it." I figured he might be intimidated by my refusal to use contractions, but no such luck.

He meowed again. I thought of the anxiety and horror he'd put me through all day long. I remembered how I'd felt trying to imagine him wandering the streets of New York City, wet, lonely, frightened. I remembered my vision of seeing Norton's picture on the side of a milk carton, with the phrase "Have you seen this cat?" All of seven seconds had passed since I'd gotten off the phone with Janis.

"Well, maybe just a snack," I allowed, and instantly opened up a can of his favorite food, scooped it into his bowl, and set it down in front of him. Grateful, Norton munched until satisfied. Then he came over and tried to get back on my good side, once and for all. The first thing he did was look me straight in the eye and start purring.

"No way," I announced. "I was given explicit instructions not to be nice to you. I can't let you starve to death, but I don't have to be friendly."

He jumped up onto the bed, looking shaken and, if truth be told, extremely pathetic. This may have been the first experience of rejection in his life. I reached out and stroked his head in a moment of forgetfulness. Norton immediately took the reassuring gesture as a sign of capitulation and he went in for the kill, rubbing his nose firmly up against my cheek, something I'm usually a sucker for. But not this time.

"Uh-uh," I told him, drawing back. "I am *not* weakening."

He now began rubbing himself against my leg.

"It's for your own good," I tried to explain. It had sounded so convincing when Janis said it.

The purring grew louder, the look in his eye more tender. My resolve, I do have to admit, was weakening rather quickly. After several minutes, when he turned over on his back and wiggled his paws around in the air, my resolve was about as firm as my backbone—which was clearly the consistency of mush.

"All right," I sighed. "C'mere."

That was it. I was a goner. Discipline was thrown out the window and I was on all fours, petting and scratching and telling him that everything was fine, I really didn't mind that he'd put me through the worst day of my life, just as long as he was okay.

This went on for quite a long time—until he was sure I'd forgiven him completely and until I was sure he understood that this hiding business was not something to be repeated in the future.

Peace made at long last, I went into the kitchen and poured myself a well-deserved beer. Then I came back to my cat and spoke two more sentences.

"Don't tell Janis," was the first thing I instructed. After all, there was no real need for her to know the extent of my wimpiness. Luckily, from the look in Norton's eye, I knew my secret soft side was safe with him. I took another long swig of beer. "And where *were* you?" was the second thing I said, very quietly.

But this time Norton only turned his head to avoid my stare. After a few moments, he glanced back at me, quietly closed his eyes, and went straight to sleep.

There are certain secrets a cat just won't share, I suppose, not even with his best friend.

3

a cat on tour

We made the decision to rent a house in Provence.

There was no particular reason for this, although we did have a certain guiding logic. We wanted to be in the country, not in a city. We didn't want to go *too* exotic since I needed to be somewhere I could get a fax machine repaired at the drop of a hat. Janis wanted warm, or reasonably warm. We wanted good food and we wanted someplace beautiful. This narrowed it down to approximately half the globe, then we got serious and started picking, choosing, and eliminating.

First we ruled out any countries with whom we didn't share an alphabet. Then we crossed off anyplace that might be under attack from Scud missiles. Next we eliminated any country that ate cats. Pretty soon, and without too much difficulty, we boiled things down to Italy and France. We winnowed out a few regions in both of those countries— Sicily was a possibility but I decided I wasn't in the mood to get blown to smithereens in my car; Burgundy was a very real consideration until Janis got it in her head that the weather was exactly like England and thus she'd be cold and damp all the time. Picture the creature in the Schwarzenegger film *Predator* and you've pretty much got Janis's personality if she was cold and damp all the time. Soon we were down to Tuscany and Provence. We compared wines and cheeses, we looked at the dollar against the lira and the franc, we did everything you were supposed to do, and then we made our decision based on one key factor: We didn't speak a word of Italian and we did speak a tiny bit of French. So we settled on Provence.

A couple of years before, while I was working with Roman Polanski on a screenplay, Norton and I'd lived in Paris for three months. Almost every night, Roman and I would go out to dinner, usually with friends of his. Roman had friends who were Italian, Polish, French, Russian, you name it. So during our meals, someone would say something in French, someone would answer in Polish, someone would then respond to that in Italian or Danish or Upper Slobovian. Every fifteen minutes or so, Roman would interrupt protectively and say, "Come on, fellows, speak English for Peter" (translation: "Come on, you guys, we've got a cretinous American here, so say something he can understand"). Rarely had I felt so inept, so when I returned to New York I was determined to learn at least one other language.

I'd had two years of high-school French, but that was so long ago I could really only remember the bare essentials. I could conjugate the verbs *aller, avoir,* and *être;* I could ask for the location of the nearest apothecary; and if someone served me the proper vegetable, I could show my appreciation by saying, *"Bravo! Des asperges!"* Braced by such a substantial background, I began taking French lessons from a rather eccentric woman who lived on the Upper East Side and who had, in a one-room apartment, six birds (including a blind pigeon she'd found in the park), one dog, three cats, and several mice (I *think* the mice were pets, though I wouldn't swear to it). She also liked to keep the room temperature somewhere near a hundred and forty degrees at all times. But I slogged through my lessons and, when the time came to *choisir un pays* (don't applaud, really), I thought my French might come in handy.

Once we'd settled on Provence, the next step was finding a house. This was something I had absolutely no concept of how to do, but I made a decent stab at it. I called the French embassy. They sent me to a French realtor with an American outlet. They in turn sent me to some company that mailed me a videotape showing all sorts of *châteaux* for sale for a mere three million dollars. I even called a realtor in France who told me that what I was looking for didn't exist and that I should stop bothering her.

Eventually, we found a house through friends of friends of friends. It sounds farfetched, but that is the absolute best way to find something. Just start telling everybody you know that you want to rent a place in the south of France. Someone is bound to say, "Oh, Fred did that two years ago. Got a great farmhouse in the country—and boy, was it cheap." It may not be in Provence—but, hey, the Dordogne ain't Pittsburgh—and the odds are that Fred's farmhouse has tripled in price since then, but it's also probable that Fred learned about other places while over there or knows somebody who knows somebody who knows somebody else who has a house for rent.

When word got out that we were looking to shove off, I got a call from a writer friend of mine. His wife was friendly with someone who lived in Paris who had a *deuxième maison* in Provence that they sometimes rented. I called the people in Paris, who told me that they were no longer renting their place out. But—and this is key; this is why it pays to talk to anyone, anytime—they loved where they lived and were very happy to find someone who also wanted to live there. So, trying to see if they could help me in some way, they asked me what I was looking for. I told them: I wanted a three- or four-bedroom house in the Lubéron. I wanted old, I wanted charming, and I wanted a garden. I also wanted something that was in a small village rather than in the middle of the countryside (Janis didn't want to feel too isolated). And we wanted something that had a few conveniences—a dishwasher and a washer-dryer would be nice—but that wasn't so modernized and Americanized that we'd feel we were renting a condo in Atlantic City. In other words, I wanted perfect. And not incredibly expensive.

Much to my surprise, they didn't tell me to rent myself a nice little room in an insane asylum, they told me they thought they could help. They had a friend who had exactly what we were looking for. They'd mention our search to her—and if she was interested, she'd get back to me.

The next day, I received an eight-page fax from a woman named Elisabeth, who turned out to not only have the perfect house but who was a classy, honorable, and generally wonderful person. Her fax described the house in great detail—it was three hundred years old, stone, four bedrooms plus an office, and it had a football-field-sized garden. It also had a dishwasher, a washer-dryer, and a BMW which we were welcome to use. She was French, her husband had been American (he'd died a couple of years earlier), so the house was half-French (the charming part) and half-Ameri-

can (the convenience part). Ooh-la-la! She stressed that it
was very countrified, although very comfortably outfitted.
"Don't expect a pancake flipper," she warned. "It's still
France." Which was okay with me. I wanted a crepe pan,
not a damn pancake flipper.

So we were all set. I had an office, Janis had a garden,
Norton had three centuries' worth of mice to chase after.
There was only one thing still left to do.

Unfortunately, to write about what it was I had to do, I
have to break a solemn vow I took with someone very near
and dear to me.

Years ago, I made a pact with my writing partner, David,
who has as much integrity and taste as it's possible to have
considering what we do to make a living. The promise we
made to each other was that we would never—artistically
speaking—eat our own entrails.

This is not nearly as repugnant as it sounds. Honest. It
simply means that when we were younger we decided that
if we ever became successful writers we wouldn't join the
Philip Roth School of Writing About How Successful We
Are. Uppermost in things to avoid: writing about how hard
it is to be a writer; writing about how no one ever appreciates how hard it is to be a writer; writing about other writers
or editors and critics, because they're all incredibly boring;
writing about how all those boring writers, editors, and
critics don't like you either; and absolutely first on the list,
never, ever, *ever* write about your own publicity tour. It's
unseemly, it's uninteresting, and it's just plain obnoxious
(as in, "Oh, yeah, sure you've got it rough over in Bosnia,
but you should have been in *my* shoes when this little short
guy with a bad rug got my *name* wrong on 'Good Morning,
Schenectady.' Now, *that* was a nightmare!'').

Anyway, Dave, I'm not really writing about *my* publicity

tour. I was all set to go over to the three-hundred-year-old house in France and keep my last few shreds of artistic dignity. I swear. Nobody wanted to talk to or see *me,* anyway. But before I could hop on a plane and hightail it out of here, I had my last little detail to take care of. It turned out that a lot of people wanted to meet my cat.

The tour officially began in Los Angeles but, in the publishing equivalent of spring training, we got a practice appearance in, on a show on a small cable station in Connecticut. Everyone thought this was a good idea since no one really knew how the cat would behave in front of the cameras and, probably more pressing, everyone wanted to see if I'd turn into the Chef of the Future once the little red light went on.

Basically, it went well. Norton was, of course, his usual perfect self. We arrived early, as instructed, and were led to the greenroom, which, in case you're interested, was brown. (Later, in several weeks of touring, I was in many, many greenrooms. Not *one* of them was ever green. I'm thinking of calling "Sixty Minutes" to see what they can do with this.) I paced the room for half an hour, looking in the mirror constantly, running my hand through my hair, straightening my tie, doing everything but going "mi mi mi" and gargling. Norton was already acting as if he'd been on as many talk shows as Teri Garr. He sat on the couch, let a few stagehands come over and pet him, and was even nice to the guest who was to follow me, a woman who'd written a book about the proper way to pack a suitcase. Ah yes, there's nothing like doing publicity to make one feel like an important cultural influence.

Once we went on the air, the host and hostess of the show couldn't get over the way Norton just sat on my lap for the whole interview. He even would sit up and look straight into the camera, thus making sure all thirty-five people watching the show would stop listening to me and pay sole attention to how cute he was. (I think he did this whenever he sensed I was going on too long and was becoming boring.)

For my part, I was fine, except that, being as vain as possible, I'd worn a dark blue suit and blue shirt, figuring that would be my best look for my TV debut. It was, I suppose, at least at the beginning. But as the show went on, Norton began doing what all cats do, especially when they're under hot lights—he began to shed. And he began to shed all over my dark blue suit. By the end of the interview, I had so much gray fur on me that I looked like nothing so much as a large, talking prehistoric bird.

But we'd not only survived the first test, it was clear that Norton was such stuff as stars were made of.

As I said, this was an early interview, a trial run. The book was still a few weeks away from being published. So all we had to do now was wait for the book to exist and then, having passed our test, wait to throw ourselves on the mercy of America.

For a writer as well as a cat, waiting is the hardest part. But, from a literary point of view, the end of the wait is usually worth it.

There is something very special about seeing one's book for the first time as a finished product. No matter the quality—whether you're Daniel Defoe or Danielle Steele—writing a book is damned difficult. Everyone *thinks* he or she can write, but it's fairly daunting to take a look at a blank page and then decide that you have the audacity to fill not only it up but many more like it. So when you finally have finished the first draft, then the second, then the third;

when you've corrected the copy-edited manuscript, then the galleys, then the bound galleys; when you finally get to hold the finished, published product in your very own hands—several hundred pages long, a real jacket, flap copy that hypes till even *your* face turns red, something solid and permanent—it provides a moment pure and satisfying. Bad reviews haven't come in yet, nor have the agent's calls telling you that three days after the pub date the book's already on the remainder tables. All that exists is this physical *thing* that somehow is a mental extension of yourself.

That lasts for all of a minute or two. Then, of course, reality comes a knockin'.

The Cat Who Went to Paris gave me a particularly satisfying couple of minutes because it was so personal and because it had extraordinarily handsome photos of my beloved companion all over the front and back jacket. The day before Norton and I were to leave on our publicity tour was the first time I saw it in a bookstore, B. Dalton's on Eighth Street down in the Village, where Norton and I were making our first public bookstore appearance that evening. I was supposed to sign books and be witty. Norton was supposed to look cute and let people admire him. I can't tell you how often, as the tour progressed, I wanted to switch roles, but everyone from the publicist to the editor to my very own girlfriend told me I'd be making a *big* mistake.

Several hours before the signing, I took Norton and we snuck into the store, incognito. (It wasn't very difficult. No one recognized me since no one had ever heard of me. And Norton's very good—when he wants to be—at slipping down into his shoulder bag and becoming almost invisible. It's why I've always thought he'd make a superb private eye.) As I casually checked the store out, trying not to look too much like an annoying author checking out the store,

I was surprised to see that the book was very well displayed—there was even a giant poster of Norton in the window. Ecstatic, I bought a copy for good luck—figuring it was probably the first hardcover sale in New York—rearranged the remaining books on the shelf so they lay face out (yes, we really do that; any writer who denies it is lying through his teeth. I didn't want the copy I bought to also be the *last* hardcover sale in New York), then practically danced back out to the street. Outside, I showed the book jacket to Norton, who seemed singularly unimpressed, perhaps wondering why I got my name on the front of the jacket but he didn't.

Later that night, we went back to the same store, boldly striding in this time, Norton fearlessly taking in the sights, both of us hoping the clerk wouldn't recognize me as the nervous, sweaty guy who'd earlier bought a copy of his own book. There were perhaps fifty people at this first signing and three speakers. The first speaker was a woman who'd written one of the all-time great cat books, *The Natural Cat.* The second speaker was a man who'd put together a superb cat encyclopedia called *The Cornell Book of Cats.* (His only flaw was that he spent *way* too much time lecturing about the tragedy of cat prostate problems. It was all I could do to keep myself—and Norton!—from passing out during that particular section of his speech. At one point, I'm afraid I did have to cover my ears and quietly hum all the words to "A Hundred Bottles of Beer on the Wall," but I'm sure no one noticed.) When it was my turn, I talked about how I came to write the book (an editor thought it was a good idea to have a book about a *bon vivant* who traveled around the world with his cat; I was so thrilled that somebody thought I was a *bon vivant,* I immediately agreed to do it), and then told several of the most amusing and amazing

Norton stories in it. Nothing was as amusing or amazing, however, as my cat's behavior during the speeches. When the first two speakers were on, Norton lounged politely, barely paying attention. When I stood up to begin, my little gray partner sat straight up on top of his table, staring right at me in rapt attention, occasionally glancing out at the audience as if to encourage them to laugh. The only problem came at the end of my talk when the cat fans in the store decided to applaud. At the first sound of enthusiastic clapping, Norton spun around so his back was to the crowd and he snuggled down out of view inside his bag. I immediately figured he didn't like my speech and was trying to discourage the positive reaction. It took me a little while to realize that, while he was otherwise totally unintimidated, the loud applause frightened him. For the rest of our tour, I would always begin my talk—even on a TV show if there was a live audience—by explaining that I had the greatest, most courageous cat in the world but that applause scared him, so could they please refrain from clapping when we were done, even on the slim chance that they felt like doing so. That made Norton much happier all along the way. And, of course, made me a bit neurotic. There's nothing like giving what you think is a slam-dunk winner of a talk, then walking off the stage to total silence. But, you know me— anything for El Foldo.

After the seminar/signing at B. Dalton, Norton and I headed back to my apartment. Still basking in the glow of our literary triumph and certain we had a big hit on our hands, I went to my phone machine to check my messages before I began packing for our next day's journey. I had only one message; it was from a middle-aged-sounding man and here it is in its extremely polite entirety:

*Uh, hello, uh, I'm looking for Peter Gethers, if this is
the same Peter Gethers who wrote a book called* The
Cat Who Went to Paris. *I'm calling all the way from
California and I bought this book for fifteen dollars. I'd
just like to say that my wife and I both read it and we'd
like our money back. This is the worst piece of shit we've
ever read. I mean it. What garbage. Total, absolute
shit. You should be ashamed. Thank you.*

In a mild state of shock, my first reaction was to wonder
which one—the man or his wife—had read it first. And
whoever did, did they then turn to their partner and say,
"Honey, I just read the biggest piece of shit I've ever read.
You've *got* to read it, too"? And then, did the other person
read it, curled up in front of a fire, turn to the first reader
and say, "Sugar pie, you're sure right with this one. Hooo-
eeee, this stinks to high heaven! Let's call the author long
distance and tell him"?

Once I decided this probably wasn't a healthy road to
pursue, I called my partner, David, to play him the message.
He didn't seem too surprised. Not because he agreed with
their assessment but because he's written several mystery
novels, one of which won an Edgar Award, and thus he's
come across his fair share of wackos. (It's a publishing rule
of thumb: Science fiction fans are absolutely the weirdest.
No question. Many of them think they're from another
planet—and, in fact, a good many of them probably are. If
you ever want to convince yourself that the nihilists are
right and that life has no meaning, go to a science fiction
convention. After the sci-fiers, though, come the mystery
fanatics. They all dress in black and have memorized everything Arthur Conan Doyle ever wrote. They also meet at

conventions two or three times a year, where they attend panel discussions on things like "What's the Best Murder Weapon?" and "Who's Zanier: Cornell Woolrich or James Cain?") David topped my anti-groupie without hesitation. He told me about one particular fan of his who called him on a regular basis, usually early in the morning before he had the wits about him to screen his calls. David described the fan as sounding a little bit too much like Hal the computer in *2001.*

"Daaave," the guy would say. "I just read your first novel again. Sixth time. And I'm gonna read it *again. Tomorrow.*" Then he'd usually say something like, "I'm in Chicago today, Dave"—a mere thousand miles from David's house. "How about I drive up and we meet for lunch?"

I felt a lot better after talking to David—demanding fifteen dollars back seemed a lot saner than a twenty-two-hour drive for lunch—and started packing for the tour. I knew enough to pack mostly gray clothes, thanks to my Connecticut experience. I also had the presence of mind to give Norton many extra Pounce that night and to pet him for a particularly long time before working up the nerve to ask him, "Do you have any idea what we're really in for?"

I don't know if he did or not, but he was certainly a good sport about it, and purred contentedly on my pillow until I fell asleep.

〜〜

The first stop was Los Angeles and the Four Seasons Hotel, home to several impressive Nortonian moments in times past.

The Four Seasons is where I always stay in L.A. It's convenient, classy, and perfect for conducting business. The staff is also extraordinarily nice to Norton. In fact, every Four

Seasons is particularly gracious toward pets. In the Boston
Four Seasons, they even have a pet room-service menu. I
know this because when we stayed there, I was happy to
find a large bowl filled with nuts when I walked into the
room. Only I soon realized they weren't nuts but dog biscuits—and fairly tasty dog biscuits, I might add. Under the
bowl was a small, printed sheet which was titled "Doggie
Delights." The rest of the menu read as follows:

BARK, BARK!

(Main Courses)

#1   Ruff, Ruff, rrr . . .
(Quickly Broiled Beef Filet with natural broth $6.00)

#2   Aowh, Aohw, Aohwooooooo!
(Boneless "Safe to Eat" Lamb Chops $7.00)

#3   Woof! Woof! Grrr!
(Roasted Chicken Breast with natural gravy $5.50)

BARK!!!

(Side dishes)

#1   Awwrr, Yip, Yip!
(Brown Rice $1.75)

#2   Grrrrrr . . .
(White Rice $1.75)

ARP! ARP!

(Assorted Ice Creams $2.00)

Needless to say, I called down to check this out. At first I
thought it was a joke, but when the room-service person

indignantly assured me it wasn't, I wanted to know why the menu was geared only for canine guests. The voice at the other end of the phone hemmed and hawed over that one but finally said he was sure that cats would also find the food quite delicious; the hotel was happy to admit that dogs were not the only four-legged connoisseurs.

It turned out the room-service maven was correct. Twenty minutes after I hung up, a waiter arrived. On the cart he wheeled in was an array of fine china. And on the china was a delicious—judging from Norton's considered reaction—chicken breast.

But even with the usual fine Four Seasons treatment, I still wasn't prepared for the greeting we got upon our arrival in L.A.

First of all, as the cab from the airport dropped me off in front of the hotel, I heard two men in black suits say, in muffled tones, "He's here." Surprised, I put the cat in his shoulder bag and we headed into the lobby. As we stepped inside, two more men in black suits said, "He's here. Get ready."

I knew Norton was popular, I thought to myself, but I felt a surprise party was just a tad excessive.

The entire lobby seemed abuzz as we walked toward the desk. There was a flurry of activity, people rushed toward me—reporters, hotel staff, more guys in black suits. I smiled broadly and Norton stuck his head out of the bag, craning his neck in his best E.T. impersonation—who are we to reject V.I.P. treatment?—and then we watched as everyone rushed toward us . . . and right past us. As even more guys in black suits stampeded by, saying things under their breath like, "Moving toward the elevator. Cover the doors," Norton and I casually glanced behind us—where the President of the United States was standing. Yup. George Bush was there for some kind of money-raising, glad-handing function. I suppose, if I'd really thought it through, I would have realized that Norton didn't need *all* of those Secret Service guys. Nonetheless, I confess to being just a tad disappointed.

Not for long, however.

With Bush out of the way, I found that cat and I were the only guests remaining in the lobby. So when I heard a woman's voice say, "Wait a second, I think he's here," I again turned behind me to see which top-notch celebrity had breezed in. Mel Gibson? Liz Taylor? The cast from "Beverly Hills 90210"? I was determined not to be sucker-punched again.

So I was even more confused when I realized there was nobody behind us, not even Herve Villachaize. Norton and I were *it* as far as lobby loiterers.

Another woman, this time from behind the check-in desk, said, quite clearly, "It *is* him. He's here!"

This led to a couple of exclamatory bursts from other women, all exceedingly attractive—one at the cashier's desk, one from behind the concierge's counter—along the lines of, "We've been waiting for you! We're *so* glad you're here!"

I decided that this was definitely more like it. Until, naturally, I was forced to accept the fact that once again I was not their obscure object of desire. The real target was not nearly so obscure.

"*Norton,*" the woman at the front desk cooed with her arms held out in welcome, "we are *so* glad to see you!"

Now, I've stayed at the Four Seasons ten or fifteen times. When I'm there by myself, they're certainly friendly—but no one ever holds her arms out to me and scratches me under the chin while shrieking how cute I look. Norton had stayed there four or five times—and no one had really even done that to *him* before. At least, not quite in this fashion. Because that night, as we checked in, just about every person who worked on the ground floor came out to fuss over their smallest, grayest guest. It turned out that the publicist for the book had sent a few copies over to the hotel several days before. They'd been passed around and read and Norton was now clearly on the Four Seasons' "A" list of desirable celebrities.

"We've upgraded you to a Four Seasons suite," the desk clerk said, smiling at the cat.

"We think you'll like it," another said, petting him.

"And we've got a few surprises for you up there," another one told him, scratching his stomach (by this time, he was lying on his back on top of the check-in counter; I was a little startled at how easily he'd succumbed to life in the L.A. fast lane).

I was starting to wonder if they were going to take Norton's credit card, since it was pretty obvious I was an afterthought, but no such luck. For that part they deigned to talk to me.

When we were finally shown to our room, we had indeed been upgraded to a suite. Norton also had a litter box already set up in the bathroom. On the floor by the TV were two elegant dishes, one for water—with a bottle of Evian next to it!—and one to fill with the cans of food that were stacked on top of the end table. And on the desk in the living room was a gift-wrapped box with a note taped to it.

Flattered and pleased, I tore open the package—only to find that it was a can of shrimp-flavored Pounce. Deflated—I don't know what I'd expected; I think I had my heart set on a lovely crystal goblet—I also opened the note, which was from the manager of the hotel. It read (handwritten):

> *Dear Norton,*
>   *Welcome back to the Four Seasons! My cats, Nicholas and Alexandra, would love to meet you someday . . . you sound like a really neat guy.*
>   *Enjoy your stay.*
>   *Kathleen Horrigan*
>   *Hotel Manager*

I prowled around the room (both rooms!), hoping that perhaps Kathy Horrigan had also left a small basket of fruit lying around for me, but not a chance. It was clear from the very beginning that Norton was the star of this little sojourn. And from his contented meowing—over by his bottle of Evian water—I could tell he was not unhappy about it.

～～～

The highlight of our travels around the country came at the very beginning of the trip in L.A. when the publisher threw a party to celebrate publication of the book. It wasn't just a regular humdrum party with potato chips and clam dip. For Norton, they threw a bash at Spago, the most famous restaurant in the country, run by Wolfgang Puck, arguably the most celebrated chef in the world.

Not that I'm jaded or anything, but I'd been to Spago plenty of times. In fact, my mother works with Wolf (she helped him write his last cookbook) and she's part of the unofficial Spago family.

Norton had never dined there, however. In fact, no cat

had ever dined at Spago before—until Norton broke the barrier that night. Broke it in style, I might add.

They closed the restaurant for a few hours for our private party. The guest of honor—a hint: not me—was given his own table, upon which he sat in a princelike fashion and let all the guests come over and pay homage. Wolf, whose renowned specialties are pizzas covered with such delicacies as smoked salmon, wild mushrooms, or caviar, made Norton a pizza covered with Norton's favorite delicacy—Pounce. The pastry chef, an amazing woman named Mary (who, in honor of an annual trip I make to Las Vegas with a bunch of friends, once made a cake in the shape of Sammy Davis, Jr.), baked small cakes and cookies with cat paws and cat whiskers all over them. I was congratulated once or twice by the fifty or so guests, but mostly they fussed over Norton. Many of them had never been out in public with him and they couldn't believe how human he acted (they thought that was a compliment; we know better). During the several hours we were there, Norton perched himself on his table/throne, ate when he felt like it, drank a little milk when he was in the mood, allowed journalists to take his picture, let children talk to him as if he were a grown-up (and I mean a grown-up person, not a grown-up cat), and permitted all his admirers to pet him, stroke him, and compliment him. He even let the manager of the restaurant repeatedly refer to him as "Norman" without swatting at his ankle.

The highlight of the evening, however, was Wolf's wife, Barbara Lazaroff, the designer of and guiding force behind Spago and all of Wolf's other restaurants. Barbara, who's extremely attractive and even more flamboyant, strode into the party wearing a cat outfit. We're talking cat slippers—

with whiskers and everything—cat pants, a cat sweater, and a cat hat. Norton, for one brief, shining moment, thought he'd met the ultimate member of the opposite sex, but eventually, to his disappointment, I'm sure, he realized that Barbara was just another admiring, if stunning, human.

After the Spago party, the rest of our tour was fairly typical—considering that one of the authors on tour was a four-legged feline. Following L.A., for the hardcover and the paperback versions of the first book about our adventures together, Norton and I went to San Diego, San Francisco, Portland, Seattle, Miami, Dayton, Rochester, Detroit, Dallas, and Philadelphia. (After the West Coast tour, I told the publisher that a city a day was just too tough on my little pal. He was an extraordinary trouper and shockingly well behaved—just ask any of the couple of thousand people who came by to meet him—but, still, I felt it wasn't fair to cart him around all day, then put him on an airplane. So, for the other cities, we were put on what I heard referred to as the "old author's tour." That meant we got an extra day or two in each city to ease the travel burden. Me, Norton, and James Michener.)

The routine was pretty much the same in each city. An escort would pick us up at the airport. I carried the portable litter boxes—I had about twenty of them in my suitcase when I started, just in case—but each escort was instructed to show up with a bag of cat litter in tow. As soon as I picked up my bags and got into the car, out would come a collapsible litter box, then I'd rip open a new sack of litter, and the whole thing would go on the floor behind the passenger seat. Then we'd get taken to our hotel. As soon as we were checked into the room, it was time for another fold-up box and more litter. This way, not only was Norton assured of never having to go too long *sans toilette,* I was assured that none of the escorts would sue me for ruining the upholstery in their Buicks.

In each new hotel room, Norton would stake out his territory. He'd prowl around, sniffing along each of the four walls. If there was a desk or chest of drawers, he'd hop up on that and check out the comfort level. If there were thick curtains, he'd disappear behind them, checking, I imagine, for scratching texture as well as hideability level (thick curtains are very nice to hide in when a noisy room-service cart careens into the room).

I had many, many cans of Norton's favorite foods and a reasonable supply of Pounce. (Although once the book came out and people read that Pounce was his favorite treat, a can of the stuff became the gift offering of choice at all autographings. On the paperback tour, Norton received, in two weeks, sixty-four cans of Pounce.) Norton's food and water were usually set down in the bathroom. I don't actually know how a cat can tell which room is a bathroom, but I do know that if he was hungry and I hadn't set down any food yet, he'd go right into the correct room and start meowing his starving head off.

San Diego was Norton's first official TV show after the Connecticut dry run. We went on "Inside San Diego," which proved once and for all that Norton had the potential to be another Lassie if he so chose.

For the entire interview he sat on my lap, not thrilled with the lights and the background noise but certainly not uncomfortable or nervous. Subdued and alert would be my description. The hostess of the show—a cat lover—couldn't get over how adorable and intelligent he seemed throughout our chat. But even she wasn't prepared for Norton's finale. As the show was ending, the director decided to put the camera on Norton as the final credits rolled. They wanted to use Camera 3 (it was a three-camera show, as are most TV interview shows) instead of Camera 1, which was the one focused on Norton during the rest of the program. Just as the countdown began to signal that the credit roll was about to start and that we'd be back on the air, the director's voice boomed from above, over the microphone linking him from the control booth to the set: "Do you think you could try to get the cat to face Camera Three?" Without missing a beat—and with no prodding or prompting from me—the newest TV heartthrob sat up on my lap, turned a hundred and eighty degrees, and made sure he was directly facing Camera 3. Just a split second before the countdown ended and the sound and cameras went on, the director summed up what he saw quite magnificently, also over the mike. "Holy shit," he said. "That cat's a fucking genius."

As we did more TV and radio, Norton became even more at ease in front of the cameras and the mikes. On various radio shows, I'd try to be my usual witty self, while Norton would sit next to me, probably wondering why he was there, since no one could see him and no one was asking him to talk. The deejay would usually exclaim, several times for his listening audience, "I know you can't see this cat, ladies and gentlemen, but he really is unbelievable!"

In San Diego, we did Michael Reagan's radio show. Much to my surprise, he turned out to be Ronald Reagan's son. I wasn't looking forward to the interview, since Reagan ranked up with Iago and Roy Cohn in my top five list of villains, but the son wound up being perfectly pleasant and funny. He also turned out to be highly allergic to cats.

The entire week before we arrived to do the show, he'd been going on the air talking about how he was dreading meeting this genius cat. He was afraid he'd be sneezing during the entire interview. Naturally, as in all cases, Norton managed to accomplish the unexpected. Not only was Reagan *not* allergic, he wound up petting him and declaring over the air that he was now going to get a Scottish Fold.

We went back to L.A. to do a Book and Author Luncheon. What happens at these lunches is that a group of book lovers, usually women, decide it would be fun and interesting to bring in two or three authors to lecture and discuss their latest works over a lunch of overcooked vegetables and undercooked chicken. I was chosen for this particular lunch and thus was up on the podium, speaking to a lot of fur-clad women, along with a woman who wrote about the emotional problems children were having in high school, a man who had an easy, step-by-step formula for everyone to reach inner satisfaction, and a woman who wrote best-selling true-crime books and lectured about the mind of the psychopathic killer. It didn't really matter what I said to this group because Norton decided to steal the show. I stood up in my nice new suit (the gray one, where all the cat hairs weren't nearly so visible), glasses perched, looking as professorial as I can, and began to talk. In the meantime, Norton decided to plop himself down right next to the podium, looking for all the world as if not only did he belong up there as one of the speakers, but as if he were, in fact, my translator. The whole time I spoke, he kept glancing back and forth between me and the audience, as if to say, "Come on, folks, he's really trying hard." Whatever I was doing, it worked. In order of popularity, I think I came in a solid third. The psychopathic killer came in second, and Norton, of course, finished first.

Seattle, Portland (it was Norton's first trip to the Pacific Northwest), and San Francisco all went as smoothly as possible. Outside of San Francisco, in Larkspur, we made an appearance at a wonderful bookstore called A Clean Well-Lighted Place for Books. The evening was sponsored by the local SPCA. I spoke, Norton sat by my side, translating as usual, and several cats found new homes. So the entire evening was a terrific success. (Not to pat myself on the back, but I do find it admirable that throughout this entire book as well as the first one, never once have I succumbed to the temptation to say things like "a purrfect success." I just wanted to point that out to anyone who felt that, in general, cat books are too cute to bear. Although I don't have any compunction about relating stories of *other* people who show overly cute tendencies in front of Norton. Once, when we were in Philadelphia, I ordered up my dinner from room service after another grueling day of being witty and charming for TV, radio, and print. When the woman from room service brought me my dinner, she couldn't help but notice Norton and give him a few friendly strokes. She left, then fifteen minutes later reappeared. This time with a bowl of cat treats and a small catnip ball. These gifts arrived with a note. The envelope was addressed to "Kitty Cat Gethers" and the note read, "Hope your stay with us is pu-u-urfect!" It was signed: "The cat lovers in Room Service." You didn't *really* think I could write an entire book like this without having one of those "pu-u-urfect" anecdotes, did you? Grow up!)

In Seattle, I did have the stupidest experience of the entire tour. What people have to understand is that while writers are thrilled to have the opportunity to promote their books, since that's the only way they can possibly hope to collect any royalties, it really ain't a lot of fun. The reason

it's not is because most of the talk-show hosts and interview-
ers who you're talking to haven't read the book and have
no idea what you're doing there with them in the first place.
At one newspaper interview in San Francisco, I went into
the reporter's office, sat down, and after he introduced
himself, I told him who I was, then pointed to the sack on
my shoulder and said, "And this is Norton." His eyes widened and he said, "You brought your *cat* to the interview????" Slightly taken aback, I shrugged and said, "Well,
yeah. He goes everywhere I go." "He *does*????" the guy
responded. "That's unbelievable." About this time, I began
to suspect that the reporter hadn't actually read the book,
so I said, "Well, see, the book's called *The Cat Who Went
to Paris* because I travel all over the world with the cat."
"And he's actually been to Paris?" the guy now asked.
"Uh-huh," I cleverly responded. "That's where we got the
title from." "Wow," the guy said, stunned at this heavy new
info. "This is unbelievable. Well . . . what do you want to
talk about?"

Some of them are bad but not quite as bad as that. One
otherwise well-done newspaper story that came out in Boston repeatedly referred to me as *Sam* Gethers (I'd spent two
hours with the reporter, but I guess I didn't really make a
big impression). I did one radio interview outside of Detroit and moments before it was was supposed to begin, the
hostess of the show rushed in, introduced herself, and said,
"We only have a minute. What's the title of the book,
what's your name, what's the book about, and what the hell
are we going to talk about?!" Refusing to panic, I calmly
gave her the title, my name, the subject of the book, and
fed her several reasonable questions to ask. We were then
given the signal that we were on the air and she began the
interview by announcing to all those listening, "I have here

today an author, Peter Gethers, who wrote a book called *The Cat Who Went to Paris*. Now, I have to be totally up front about this: I hate cats and I hate cat books."

One good thing about that opening: The interview had nowhere to go but up.

Throughout the entire tour, Norton behaved impeccably. Rarely did he stumble and start to act like a . . . well . . . like a cat. I think he was fairly exhausted by the end, as was his dad, but generally he got to eat a lot, sleep a lot, and have tons of people tell him he was the greatest thing that ever walked the earth. So, while I was glad to get him back home, where he could curl up in his favorite and familiar spots, I think he had a fine time overall on the road.

In San Francisco, I realized he'd just about had it, though, when, one day at a radio interview, he decided to hide.

When I was being interviewed, he'd usually sit right by my side, but this afternoon he was restless. The interviewer, a woman named Ginnie Waters, who hosted a show on KKSF Radio called "Something Different," loved cats and encouraged Norton to stroll around the little broadcast booth as much as he wanted. Since he'd been absolutely purrfect . . . uh, perfect (sorry) . . . for the entire tour, and this was the very last stop for a while, I relaxed and didn't bother to keep my eye on him. The interview took half an hour, went quite well, and when it was over, I called for Norton to come and hop into his shoulder bag. Only there was no Norton. I knew I was in trouble because he'd been a little cranky all day. I should have seen it coming—he'd had a tough trip and was just plain tuckered out—but his timing was not great. For one thing, we had a plane to catch. For another, I'd just spent half an hour telling a good chunk of San Francisco about what an extraordinary cat he was and now I had to spend another half an hour crawling around

on my stomach, peering under desks, climbing up on
shelves, and searching through strange electronic equipment, while a bemused member of the media watched me
try to find my cat. Finally, I heard a meow—he'd decided
to let me know he was okay—but there was still no cat in
the booth. He meowed again—and kept meowing for another fifteen minutes—but I absolutely could not find him.
It wasn't until one of the engineers came in and suggested
I look inside one of the speakers that the hiding place was
discovered. How he managed to get in there, none of us
could figure out. But, cat extraordinaire that he was, he'd
managed to slip into the one place in a ten-by-ten room
where he couldn't possibly be spotted. He didn't resist
when I picked him up, and I sure didn't scold him. He
wasn't angry; he wasn't even really hiding. He was just
letting me know, in his own inimitable way, that he'd had
enough. And I sure couldn't blame him.

But none of this holds a candle to the moment in Seattle.
It came at exactly 6:05 A.M. Now, I'm not really the greatest morning person. I can survive it, but I'd gotten into
Seattle about 10 P.M. the night before and, between one
thing and another, hadn't gotten to sleep until well after
midnight. So I wasn't thrilled about getting up at five, slurp-
ing down a cup of coffee, and then waiting for the radio
station to call me in my room for their morning phoner.
Reliable author that I am, however, I did it with as big a
grin on my mug as I could muster. And, sure enough, just
as I was stifling a major yawn, the phone rang and it was the
drive-time radio show. They told me to hold on a couple
of minutes while they did the traffic report and then they'd
get back to me. So I yawned and held on and eventually
heard a typical frenzied deejay's voice saying, "And in just
a moment, we'll be talking to Peter Gethers, author of *The*

Cat Who Went to Paris, and his amazing cat, Norton. Hello, Peter . . . are you there?" I told him I was here—and he then asked, in his best slick radio cadence, "Tell me, Peter, what does Norton think of relationships in the nineties?"

I should say right now that I'm usually a fairly glib person. It takes a lot for me to be stumped. Maybe it was the fact that it was the middle of the night, as far as I was concerned. Maybe it was that we'd been touring for too many days in a row. But all I could think of to say was a not-very-glib, *"What?"* And when he repeated the question, I came back with, "Uh . . . well . . . he approves of them."

"Thank you very much," I heard. "That was Peter Gethers, author of *The Cat Who Went to Paris,* and his amazing cat, Norton, on relationships in the nineties." And then he hung up.

I decided I had nobody to blame but myself, wondered how Tolstoy would have responded if he'd been out promoting *Anna Karenina*—"Tell me, Leo, what does Count Vronsky think about relationships in the 1800s?"— then got dressed, kissed the cat, and went on to our next interview.

The best part of being on tour was going to bookstores. Not only was it exciting to see truly great stores—and once again be reminded why I do what I do to earn my keep— it was extraordinarily fun to see how people reacted to Norton.

One woman at the Boston University bookstore showed up at a signing with photos of her family—which consisted of *six* Scottish Folds.

Two women who came to meet Norton at the Village

Green in Rochester were Scottish Fold breeders who appeared with their impressive brochures filled with cute photos of Fold kittens. These two charming women, Barbara Meyers and Grace Sutton, are responsible for the fact that Esther, my agent and lifelong die-hard resister of cats, finally gave in and now has a folded-eared pal of her own named Tate.

When I would sign books, people lined up for books while I sat behind a table and Norton sat on the table. Someone would hand me a book, ask me to sign it (scarily enough, often to someone named Fluffy, Spitball, Pooh, or Peanut Butter), and while I was doing so, he or she would pet Norton, coo over him, and, as often as not, hand him a can of Pounce as a present (one woman tentatively presented me with some M&Ms because she felt guilty that I wasn't getting enough attention; other than that, I was strictly in the background).

If someone had never heard of the book but just happened to be wandering by, they'd usually give me a perfunctory glance, spot Norton doing his shtick, widen their eyes, then sidle over to me to ask a few questions. The questions would usually range from "Is he a trained cat?" (Answer: No) to "Why does he look so funny?" (Answer: It's the breed) to "He's so calm. Did you drug him?" (Answer: No!) to "Did you clip his ears?" (Answer: NO!!!!).

At Gene's Books in King of Prussia, Pa., they had a photo contest. People brought in a picture of their own cute feline and I was supposed to pick winners in the following categories: Fattest Cat, Most Amazing Cat, and Cutest Cat. This was not unlike being put in the delicate situation of having to choose which person's baby is better looking. I did my best, being careful not to always choose photos of Folds, since I didn't want to appear to be too biased. Overall, the winners were gracious and the losers didn't either hit me or tear up my book, so I suppose it could be considered a successful contest.

At Liberties Books and Fine Music in Boca Raton, Florida, people were encouraged to bring their own cats to meet Norton. One guy brought a large St. Bernard dog, for some strange reason, and one couple brought a large black cat who was the calmest cat I've ever seen. Norton, when he's in public, is not particularly nervous or hyper, but he does stay extremely alert. If I lecture for more than half an hour, he may doze off, or may turn over on his back, purr, and demand to be scratched, but usually he sits calmly, checking out the situation, making sure that there aren't going to be any unpleasant surprises. But this black cat didn't care about surprises or anything else that I could see. He simply sat in the audience and was about as tense as a bowl of jello. One of his owners brought the cat over to meet me—and the cat was hanging upside down from the guy's hands like a side of beef in a meat locker. I couldn't tell if Norton was a little jealous or if he was merely scornful of the black cat's eagerness to please. I like to think it was the latter, as I presume he's above any feeling of petty jealousy, but he was definitely standoffish toward this feline competitor.

At Books & Co. in Dayton, Ohio (the country's second largest independent bookstore and a book lover's fantasy), I was the second speaker of the evening. The only problem with that was, while the first speaker was going on—her book and talk were both quite charming, all about various American family traditions—Norton and I stood off to the side, preparing for our own little seminar. So while this other poor author was speaking, people started spotting the cat and coming over to pet him and say hello. Pretty soon, there were fifty people surrounding Norton, praising him to the skies, while three people were left sitting in front of the family traditions woman. I got the distinct impression, when we were both dropped off at our hotel later that night, that her family's newest tradition was going to be hating authors who write books about their cats.

In Dallas, not only did Norton finally get his first taste of real barbecue, he was now so relaxed about appearing on television that he actually fell asleep on a local talk show. The setup was vaguely "Tonight Show"-ish—the host sat in a chair while the guests lined up along a couch. Norton and I were the only guests. He sat closest to the interviewer and I sat next to him. The woman who was the star of the show was a fanatical cat lover and I think she was never really sure to whom she should address her questions, me or Norton. Every so often, I could see a look of surprise on her face after she'd ask something and I was the one who responded. The whole time I was talking, I was rubbing Norton, until somewhere in the middle of the interview, the host said, "Well, I can see the problem with Norton is that he's just too tense under the scrutiny of public life." I looked down and, sure enough, the Perry Como of the feline world had his head tucked into his body, all curled up in a ball, and he was sound asleep, purring away. By the time we got to Taylor's Bookstore the next day, I could tell that Norton was beginning to take seriously to the celebrity life. As the hundred or so people lined up to meet him, I had the distinct impression that he was disappointed there were no cameras around to record his every movement (which, I must admit, weren't many; mostly he would stick his head up to be scratched or stick his head down to be hand-fed a couple of treats. He's kind of a minimalist when it comes to actual public activity).

When the tour for the hardcover book was over, I believe that Norton felt much as I did. There was a sense of relief—it was nice to be home rather than in a new hotel room every day, and it was even nicer to be alone, without having to constantly be performing, something neither writers nor cats take to naturally or are great at. At the same time, there was a little bit of a letdown. For a short burst of time, we were center stage. Don't panic, neither one of us ever fully turned into Sally Field at the Academy Awards, but I do think there was a slight addiction to the public acclaim. Cats and writers are both loners for the most part and there was something gratifying, however uncomfortable it sometimes felt, about people personally acknowledging that we had given their lives some pleasure.

I believe, after the tour ended, that Norton had a slightly different relationship with the human race. Prior to this experience, I was basically the one who'd provided him with the most protracted and strongest feelings of affection and love. Several girlfriends over the years adored him and let him know it, and he'd met all of my friends, who fussed over him more than enough to keep him happy. In our various travels, he'd also encountered plenty of strangers who certainly pumped up his ego. But on this trip it was the first time he was able to sense that *many* people, *thousands* of people, wanted to love him. If not him specifically, then something—or someone—very much like him.

It was an interesting switch. Cats often affect people in strange and mysterious ways and, for the most part, change our lives for the better. It's what they do. It's one of the things that makes them cats. But this was a rare occasion when people were able to substantially change a cat.

Since Norton can't really talk—even though I'm able to interpret many of his meows, it's fairly difficult to have a philosophical conversation with him—I can't be absolutely certain that this change was as strong as I suspect. But I can turn the tables on my cat and observe him, sit back and watch him in action, and I *am* certain, from my observations after the tour, that he was different after coming in contact with so many people who so clearly adored him, and who just as clearly yearned for him to adore them.

He certainly didn't turn into a lap dog. God forbid. Nor did he lose any of his independence or his individualistic spirit. But I noticed that when a stranger came in the room and reached out a hand, Norton's neck would move just an inch in the proper direction, an admission, however grudgingly, that love was not a one-way street.

For a cat, that ain't bad.

And for a cat, an author, and an author's girlfriend, it also meant it was time to put our past lives behind us and head off across the Atlantic.

PART TWO

a
cat
abroad

4

a cat in france

Then there was the bad weather.

Just kidding—that's the opening line to *A Moveable Feast*. I always like to see who's on their toes.

Unlike Papa, as I call him, when we arrived in Paris the autumn weather was absolutely spectacular. Getting there was not quite as pleasant, however.

One of the drawbacks of giving up the life of semi-high-powered publishing executive was that I also gave up the semi-high salary that went along with that life. Saving money just happens not to be my strong point (I'm much, much better at spending it), so, trying to show me that a careful, considered, budget-conscious life could also be fun and rewarding, Janis convinced me to get tickets using our American Advantage Miles. In other words, we could fly to France for free.

I don't know how many of you have ever tried to actually order whatever Advantage Miles are due you. But let me assure you, if you don't have a Ph.D in Reading Instructions, give it up. Don't bother. As a publisher, I had to wade my way through many a complicated contract. I know all about options and step deals and various parties of the first part and even something about a few parties of the second part, but trying to order Advantage Miles was something substantially beyond my intellectual capabilities. I couldn't figure out how many miles it took to get an international flight. Then I couldn't figure out how many more it took to get a seat in business class. Then, to make matters worse, I absolutely couldn't figure out what dates were restricted or what dates were okay to fly. The nearest I could come was that, with the mileage I'd accumulated, I could either fly nonstop to Asia or I could get an upgrade on a flight to Seattle, but I couldn't fly anywhere else unless I wanted to go after two A.M. on the eighteenth day of every other month. After several hours of trying to make sense of the back of my Advantage Miles statement, and finally realizing that whatever I did was going to be one hundred percent incorrect, I called American Airlines and threw myself on the mercy of whoever answered the phone. I promised them that I was a reasonably intelligent person who normally could function in the real world, and then I confessed that trying to figure out their simple system for free flights was the equivalent, for me, of those spatial-relations tests they used to give in junior high school. Sometimes I still wake up screaming as I remember sitting at my desk, looking at a drawing of two gears, and staring at the caption which read: *If the gear on the right spins counterclockwise and strikes the gear on the left, which way will the gear on the left turn?* Not since those mind-numbing sessions—where I would spend the entire hour twisting myself into a pretzel trying desperately to figure out the proper movement, then trying even more desperately to even figure out what a gear *was,* after which my friendly counselor suggested that I try to stay away from all activity that ever involved any form of mechanical skill or abstraction—had I felt the way I felt reading those Advantage Mile forms.

My only consolation was that the woman at the airline was very understanding, leading me to believe that at least some other customers had run into the same roadblock I had. Not many, but some.

We finally figured out what I needed to know and our tickets were ordered. But after this was all done, Janis asked if I'd made a reservation for Norton. I hadn't yet—that had to be done separately; I was afraid of overloading my sympathetic airline friend—but I assured her it would be no problem.

As usual, I was completely wrong. It was a huge problem. American Airlines no longer allowed pets to fly in the cabin on international flights.

This was absurd, and I said as much to whoever I talked to at the American reservation desk. That may be, she said, but it was also company policy. So I asked to speak to the manager. He was quite nice and friendly, but he also told me it was company policy. But, I argued, I fly American everywhere in the States just because they let me take my cat in the cabin with me. Yes, he assured me, that was correct. But not for international flights. When I asked why that was, he told me it was the law.

Granted, I'm not a lawyer, but I seriously doubted there was a law on the books that forbade cats to fly with their owners from New York to Paris. I was also fairly sure it was nowhere to be found in the Constitution of the United States. And while I knew that such a right wouldn't be covered in the Bill of Rights (I can see it now—Thomas

Jefferson stroking his chin, deep in thought . . . "Hmmm.
Let's see . . . let's give everyone the right to freedom of
speech . . . the right to privacy . . . I know! And the right
to bear cats on airplanes!"), I had a distinct feeling that this
guy from American was not telling me the truth. So I did
what any normal, cat-loving person would do. I called the
president.

Give me a break—not the President of the United States.
I'm not a total lunatic. But I did call the prez of American
Airlines. I explained to him that I had just written a best-
selling book about traveling around the world with my cat,
that I was going to be writing another, and that, for some
weird reason, his airline, which was always so nice to my
little furry friend, would not allow him to fly with me to
Charles de Gaulle Airport. I'm a little ashamed to mention
it, but sometimes this mention of the book works when all
else fails. Once, when Norton and I went down for our
annual spring training trip to Florida, the Rotisserie Baseball guys who organized the trip decided to change from
our usual hotel. No more Belleview Biltmore, where they
loved the cat—despite the time he fell fifteen feet through
the dining-room awning and almost gave two seventy-five-
year-old women heart attacks when he landed on their
table. We were now staying at a large, pink monstrosity
called the Don Cesar. Because Norton had been going on
this baseball trip for so many years, it never occurred to me
to make a reservation for him, which turned out to be
unfortunate because the Don Cesar didn't take cats. I won't
give all the gory details, but there was no chance of getting
into another hotel within a hundred miles, so I wound up
sneaking Norton into my room. The next morning, the
manager of the hotel accosted me, drawing himself up to his
full height of five feet six inches, and telling me that he

heard I had a cat in my room. I stared him straight in the
eye—I had to stoop a bit—and, looking as indignant as
possible, lied my head off. Later that morning, when I returned to my room after breakfast, who was there but the
manager, snooping around. Not only did he find the litter
box, the cat food, and the bowl of water, he found the cat.
I tried being outraged that he'd broken into my room, but
it's hard to sustain outrage when you're caught in a total lie.
So I did the next best thing: I offered to bribe him. When
that didn't work, I became desperate and told him that I had
a book coming out in several months, that the book was
expected to be a best-seller, and that if he didn't let my cat
stay there, I'd make sure I wrote terrible things about him
and the hotel in the book. Even Norton was embarrassed
by this feeble attempt to keep him sheltered, but much to
our shock, it worked. The manager suddenly looked at
Norton, smiled somewhat sycophantically (a trait I personally like in hotel personnel), and said that Norton certainly
looked like an extraordinary cat and he didn't see what
harm a feline could do for just a few days. Now I know how
it feels to abuse the power of the media. It feels just *great!*

However, such a ploy didn't work with American Airlines. The president (to be honest, he was sort of vague
about his title; he never actually *told* me he was the president even though that's who I asked to be connected to. My
own opinion is that he was a fake president, someone they
use when dealing with crackpots on the telephone) told me
that the several people I'd already talked to were absolutely
correct. It was against company policy to fly a cat in the
cabin internationally. "Why is that?" I asked as politely as
possible. "I think it's against the law," he told me.

At this point, I had visions of a major Supreme Court
case. *Norton* v. *the United States of America.* It had a nice ring

to it. I was already beginning to fantasize about Clarence Thomas catching Norton alone in a hallway and making a pass, but, as always, Janis pulled in the reigns on my sanity and convinced me that it would be a lot easier to simply get a ticket on another airline.

So on the day of our departure, Janis flew for free on American Airlines. Norton and I flew—not even remotely for free—on Air France. I was not unhappy paying for the flight, since there was no way Norton was ever flying in the baggage compartment. And for some reason—and this will definitely be brought up when I appear before the Supreme Court—it is not illegal for Air France to fly their cats in comfort and plush surroundings up with their two-legged customers, only for American-based airlines.

Norton and I had a delightful flight. I'd found a brand-new traveling kennel for him. Instead of those hard, heavy cases that fit under the seat but force him to assume a pancakelike position for much of his air time, I'd discovered these wonderful shoulder bags made out of a very tough cloth and which are airline approved. There's mesh in the back, so Norton can look out, and it unzips, so he can even stick his head out, which is his favorite way to travel. For takeoffs and landings, the thing zips up and fits under the seat, but it's extremely comfortable and makes Norton's trips a lot more luxurious.

Of course, on Air France, they are incredibly nice to a certain Scottish Fold, and this trip was no exception. The business-class cabin was nearly empty, so Norton got his own seat, as well as his own meal of smoked salmon and baked *lotte.* All in all, he was quite a hit on the flight. A very attractive and very French woman sat next to me, curled up in a little ball under a blanket. When she saw Norton up on my lap, she squealed and said, "Oh, ees he an American

Curl? I joost saw one of zose." I did my best to explain the concept of Scottish Fold—which, in French, translates vaguely into *Écosse Plier*—but I don't think it really came across. Norton's personality did come across to the two stewardesses, who spent an inordinate amount of time making sure that he was comfortable and well-fed. As we taxied into Charles de Gaulle, one of the attendants made the following announcement over the loudspeaker: "Please remember to take all packages weeth you. Except for ze passengaire in fourteen A. Eef he would like to leave his leetle cat, Norton, we would be very glad to take care of heem. Sank yoo."

~~~

Janis and I decided, due to several factors—the number of suitcases we had (whenever we moved, I felt exactly like the elder Charles Foster Kane: baggage stretched out for miles before us); our impatience to get started with our new lives in the house we'd rented down in Provence; the fact that Paris costs several million dollars per minute—not to dawdle in the city for too long. We were headed to the countryside, so to the countryside we decided to head.

We stayed at a friend's apartment for the night, determined to get an early start in the morning. Once we were over our jet lag and had our espresso and croissant the next morning, the first thing that had to be done was to pick up the car we'd rented. One nice thing about moving abroad for a year is you learn all about these strange businesses and services that, ordinarily, you'd never discover. One such business was something called Europe by Car. Instead of renting a European Ford from Avis at a cost of thousands of francs a week, Europe by Car leases Citroëns and Peugeots for up to six months at a time at a very reasonable rate.

We'd ordered a brand-new, shiny red Citroën for ourselves, and all I had to do was go pick it up.

Easier said than done in Paris.

Janis stayed at the apartment; Norton and I headed for
some strange part of south Paris that we'd never been to
before. I don't think too many other people had been there,
either. And those who were wandering the streets all
looked like they were trying to collect the reward for killing
Salman Rushdie. I did manage to find the garage eventually, and once that was done also managed to polish off all
the paperwork and other rigamarole one has to do. Then
I was pointed toward another room, followed instructions,
and went to get my car.

A very Parisian auto mechanic—overalls, a beret, a thick
black mustache; he looked like he'd fix your transmission
with a loaf of bread rather than a wrench—insisted on showing me all the fine points of my new vehicle before letting
me drive off. I tried to tell him that I had a hard time
understanding car talk in English, let alone French, but he
paid me no mind. I vaguely followed his explanations of the
clutch and the trunk and the hand break, and Norton
seemed satisfied with the seating room in the back, which
of course was of primary importance, but my interest really
perked up when he pointed to some little lever to the right
of the driver's seat.

"Ne touchez pas, monsieur," he told me. *"Ne touchez
jamais."*

"Why shouldn't I ever touch it?" I asked back.

He gave me one of those French looks. The look that
says, "Why do Americans insist on asking questions when
all that is called for is simple truth?" And he wagged his
finger at me, looked down at the lever, and repeated his

words of warning. *"Ne touchez pas,"* he said and shook his head solemnly.

"But what does it do?" I asked.

He looked at me incredulously. *"C'est très important,"* he whispered. The whispering meant it was even more important than I'd already suspected. *"Ne . . . touchez . . . pas."* There was a good ten-second pause before he added the word I knew was coming. *"Jamais."*

I decided to give it one more shot.

"I promise I won't touch it," I said. "I swear. But just give me a hint. What does it do?"

My French mechanic zipped up the front of his overalls, wiped his hands on his pant leg, and walked over to me. He put his hands on my shoulder and stared me straight in the eye.

"Monsieur," he said, in a tone worthy of a head of state announcing the commencement of war. "I would like to say just one thing to you."

"I think I know what it is," I told him.

He spun around, took two steps toward the exit, then spun back around to me. He held out his arm, extended a finger of his hand, and pointed toward the lever in the car.

"Ne touchez pas," he ordered.

"Jamais?" I asked.

Pleased—but still grave and unsmiling—he nodded. *"Jamais,"* he agreed, and left for lunch.

I never did *touche* that lever. I also never found out what the hell it was for. All I know is, for the rest of the year, I lived in mortal fear that a stranger would get behind the wheel of that red Citroën, spot an interesting lever to his right, and either some poor passenger would be catapulted through the roof or some city in China would actually be wiped off the face of the earth.

Of much more immediate concern, however, was getting back to Janis and the apartment where we'd left her.

Aside from my lack of mechanical ability, I have possibly the world's worst sense of direction. I can get lost in New York City—where the streets are arranged numerically!— so driving in Paris turned out to be somewhat of an adventure. All streets in Paris are one way, usually going exactly the opposite direction from the one I wanted to go, and very few streets go for more than a block or two without turning into another name. Which makes it very difficult to get around if you don't know where you're going. It's hard enough driving and simultaneously reading a map, but it's especially hard in Paris, where every two seconds someone either's honking at you or screaming at you or trying to get you to buy some pastry.

I did learn one very important lesson, however: Cats may be wonderful at many, many things, but reading maps is not one of them.

It took me two and a half hours to make the twenty-minute drive to the apartment. But once there, we were all packed and, once Janis was placated, we were also ready to move out.

And so, only a few hours behind schedule, we began our drive down south.

Norton had never been through the Loire Valley—the Valley of Kings—and for that matter neither had Janis, so we decided to spend a few days meandering through that region's *châteaux* and drinking its superb wine.

Once we finally figured out how to get out of Paris (I don't think I can stand to recount how many times I actually had to drive around the roundabout at the Arc de Triomphe; let's just say it was not a pretty sight), we decided to drive the ninety kilometers to the town of Chartres and begin there.

Perhaps you have picked up on the fact that I am not, in any way, shape, or form, a religious man. I relate to my own culture as I relate to most every other culture—through its food and its women. Thus, except when I once dated a dental hygienist named Rachel, a satisfying Sunday brunch of lox and bagels is about as close as I get to any sort of mystical experience involving my own heritage. Other religions and religious rites leave me cold, too. I'm not much of a believer in spectacle (I can pass just as easily on the Rose Bowl Parade as on midnight mass at St. Patrick's). Neither fear nor guilt work well for me as motivating forces, and I've never thought much of dressing up in long, flowing robes, heavy crowns, and millions of dollars' worth of jewelry except to think that the Pope and Allan Carr would probably have a lot to talk about. I don't believe in heaven or hell (unless you count Anaheim) and I don't think praying for one's soul does any good other than to absolve one from an awful lot of responsibility. I sort of understand the fatalism of various Eastern religions, but I can't say I see much sense in climbing incredibly steep mountains just to find inner peace. I can do that watching Dwight Gooden throw a perfect Lord Charles. As far as walking over hot coals and doing the thing where you sleep on a bed of sharp nails, ix-nay on that. Redemption in the form of pain *really* doesn't cut it with me. All in all, I can't say I believe in god. If, in fact, I ever find out that he does indeed exist, I think I'll stay away from him, because if he's responsible for half the things he gets credit for, he's got to be one mean son of a bitch.

To walk into the cathedral at Chartres, however, makes one understand religion and everything that created it. It's not as if I feel that god was behind this remarkable structure, but it's impossible not to feel the power that *was* behind it—that power being the *belief* in god.

There has been a church at the site of the current cathedral since the fourth century, though the cathedral that stands now wasn't built until 1194. Well, at least it was begun in 1194, and was finished, remarkably, in only thirty years. I am not a student of architecture and this book is not meant to be used as a travel guide, but to stand before the church's facades, the flying buttresses, the *Clocher Neuf,* the overwhelmingly beautiful thirteenth-century stained glass and the fourteenth-century stone choir screen is really to stand before the beauty and power of history. It is as overwhelming a visual experience as I can imagine.

Norton seemed quite floored as well. The three of us toured the inside of the cathedral—Norton on my shoulder, as usual—then sat in a pew to rest and try to absorb what we were looking at. Usually, in such situations, Norton will either be oblivious to his surroundings—i.e., sleeping the sleep of all cats—or he'll be looking every which way, trying to see everything that can be seen, as well as keeping an eye out for any potential dog alerts. At Chartres, however, Norton sat on the pew, head up, and very slowly swiveled his neck, looking first at the huge organ, then studying the pulpit, then taking in the sculptures and paintings and thousands of candles. At one point, a representative of the church ambled over to us and started to say something—I'm fairly sure what he was trying to articulate was that cats weren't allowed in places of worship—but then he saw Norton respectfully eyeing the carved wooden archway to our right, so he ambled back from whence he came. It looked to me as if he realized the cat was appreciating what he was seeing just as much as any other tourist, and he decided the no-cat rule probably wasn't apt in this instance. If only he'd worked for American Airlines instead of god, my life—and probably the lives of countless others—would have been a lot easier.

Going from the splendor of the cathedral to the backseat of the red Citroën, Norton was clearly psyched for his first car trip through the French countryside.

Our next stop was the splendid town of Amboise. Amboise is known for several things: It's where Leonardo da Vinci was buried in 1519; it's where the Mona Lisa was first brought to France; it's where Charles VIII died after hitting his head on a very low doorway. (I'm not making that up! And that would definitely rank near the bottom of ways I personally want to leave this earth.) It's also where Norton jumped out of his shoulder bag and ran away for the only time in his life.

Amboise is down by the river and its amazing *château* is terraced high above it. Before touring the castle, we decided to explore the town, since my favorite thing in France is simply to walk around, watch the people, and stop into as many *pâtisseries* as possible. Janis likes to see how many museums and ruins she can visit in one day; my idea of being a tourist is to find an atmospheric café and spend the day sipping espresso and pretending to be French. For this, our first day in the Loire, we decided to compromise. We'd take the *château* tour, but first I got to walk, drink, eat, and pretend. Norton, of course, accompanied us everywhere. Strolling, sightseeing, caféing. He was right at home.

At one point, we decided to stop at the post office to send back a few postcards. The Amboise *bureau de poste* was in the busiest part of town. After we'd bought our stamps and done our mailings, we headed back to the old town, but before we got there, a large truck decided to barrel past us, its horn blaring, at the exact same time that a bicycle decided to nearly sideswipe me and knock me into the bushes. I was a little unnerved—mostly by the jarring honk from the truck, which wasn't all that close, just loud—but nothing seemed out of place until I heard Janis scream. I turned back to see what she was screaming at, reached into the shoulder bag to make sure Norton was okay, and then realized why she was shrieking—because Norton had jumped out of the bag and was streaking off down the street. He was already a good twenty feet away from us and running as fast as he could. Before Janis could even get out the words "Go get him!" Norton had rounded a corner and disappeared into the heart of a medieval hill town.

I will say one thing for my relationship with my cat—at no time have I ever condescended to him. I refuse to believe he would ever do anything completely untoward. I don't mean something annoying like hiding for the day, I mean something permanently improper—like running away.

Janis, on the other hand, panicked. She kept yelling for me to chase after him, even after I pointed out that even in my best years, I could not run fast enough to catch a cat who didn't want to be caught. Instead, I took a deep breath and told Janis that he would be waiting calmly for me to come get him around the next corner.

Still calm, I led her to the street down which Norton had disappeared. Together we walked—not ran but walked, albeit with a fairly quick stride—the two hundred feet or so to the next corner . . . and there, sitting in the middle of the street, waiting for us, was Norton. He had quietly planted himself in front of a dry cleaner's and had an expression on his face that, without a doubt, was meant to convey, "So where were you? I've been waiting."

He sat there until I went right over to him, picked him up, and set him back in his bag.

Janis merely scowled and shook her head.

"He won't run away," I told her.

"Yeah, well *I* might," she said.

I stroked my cat, gave him a quick look, which I'm sure he knew meant I'd been a lot more worried than I'd let on, and then we went up to see the Amboise *château.*

It was spectacular. Even Norton thought so (although every time he shifted in his bag to get a better look at his surroundings, Janis practically jumped out of her skin). We saw Leonardo's tomb and the plans and models of his early inventions (how is it that someone was able to sketch plans for an airplane and automobile in the early 1500s and I can't touch my fax machine without getting a paper cut that slices my finger practically to the bone? It doesn't seem fair). We also got our first inkling of how far we had to go with our grasp of the French language.

We'd decided to take a tour of the place, led by a woman who explained—in French—what we were seeing. She was obviously well schooled when it came to tourists because, realizing that very few of us were linguists, she spoke ve . . ee . . rr . . yy . . . sllooowwwllyy. I thought I was doing rather well, following almost everything, until afterward I asked Janis what in the world the guide was talking about when she told us the story about the shoemakers.

"*What* shoemakers?!" Janis demanded.

"You know," I said. "The shoemakers in the forest who

ran around and—here's where I'm a little fuzzy—found shoes and brought them back for the king?"

I'll actually never forget the expression on my darling's face (or, as they say in France, on the face of my *petit chou-chou*—my little brussels sprout) when she realized to what I was referring. It was a look that combined astonishment, awe, and not a little bit of terror.

The guide had told this long, I thought convoluted story, about the *chasseurs* going out to do their thing for King François Premier (or, François the First to you). I couldn't begin to fathom why *chasseurs*—which I thought were shoemakers—would go searching for pumps and loafers in the woods. It turns out that cha*u*sseurs are shoemakers. And they weren't foraging for leather goods in the king's backyard. Ch*a*sseurs are *hunters.* And they weren't bringing back boots for Frankie either, they were bringing him wild game that they'd shot. To say I missed the point would be a slight understatement, especially since my slant on the entire rest of the guide's story revolved around this whole shoe issue. I was particularly bewildered about the annual "Feast of the Open-Toed Sandals."

Oh, well. So I wasn't ready to resume my dinners with Polanski et al. and seize control of the conversation. Soon, I assured my two traveling companions. But neither Janis nor Norton looked convinced.

I *was* ready—and so was at least one of them—to drink some wine. So we began the *dégustation* part of our Loire trip.

The first place we stopped was Azay-le-Rideau, which in addition to delicious white wine, had a world-class castle. We hit a few *caves,* sampled the local *vin,* then took Norton to see his second *château.* I remembered going to Azay-le-Rideau nearly twenty years before, and I was positive that the word then was that this was the place where the Sleeping Beauty legend grew up.

"Just think," I kept saying to Janis, "this is where Sleeping Beauty was supposed to have slept."

"Prove it," Janis kept saying back to me, because, sure enough, nowhere—in any guide book or anywhere at the castle—was this rather wonderful fact mentioned.

"That's the problem with the modern world," I muttered, when I realized it was my word against Michelin's. "No romance."

"Maybe some shoemakers used to come here," Janis told me, but I made sure she knew that that tack was not going to make me feel any better.

We wound up spending three more days touring *châteaux* and beautiful Loire towns. We never planned ahead, just took our chances on finding a hotel. Twice we went for local dives, which were just fine; once we stayed in a converted castle. Norton liked that room best of all, because it had a beautiful large red satin chair that he used to much the same effect as a throne.

The first couple of hotels we stayed in, I followed the same routine. I'd pull up in front, have Janis wait in the car with you-know-who, then I'd timidly ask the desk clerk or innkeeper if they would let a cat spend the night. Each time, I got exactly the same response.

"Why not?" was the standard reply. "We'd let *you* stay here. Why wouldn't we let a cat stay here?"

I must say, I thought this attitude remarkably healthy, and so, obviously, did Norton. Not only did he make himself comfortable in each room we spent the night, he came down to dinner with us also, and generally had the run of each establishment.

We took Norton to some of the most beautiful places in

France over these few days. We went to the *château* in Blois. (Two interesting facts about Blois: The first is that the name of the town is Celtic and it means "wolf"—and, by the way, so does almost everything else in French; anywhere we'd go for dinner, we'd ask what the name of the restaurant meant and at least fifty percent of the time it was some ancient language for "wolf." The second is that the entire town smells like chocolate. Don't ask me why. I will just assume there's either a large chocolate factory nearby or a really, really fat person with no willpower lives there.)

Norton toured the *château* in Chambord, which looks English to me, perhaps because it was a famous hunting lodge in the 1500s, as well as Cheverny, which still has much of its original furnishings, and he was definitely the first cat since the time of Henry II to tour the two most amazing *châteaux* in the Loire, Chinon and Chenonceau.

Chinon, for those of you who know their history from movies rather than reality, is where Peter O'Toole imprisoned Katharine Hepburn in *The Lion in Winter*. It is mostly in ruins but, perhaps more than any other structure in all of France, strikes me absolutely dumb. It sends shivers up and down my spine. Part of it, I'm sure, is my overactive imagination. Nonetheless, the ruins and history of Chinon inspire dreams and fantasies unlike anyplace I've ever seen.

Chinon is where Joan of Arc stopped to meet the Dauphin—and miraculously recognized the heir to the throne, even though he was dressed a lot like Red Skelton in the guise of Freddie the Freeloader. When Janis, Norton, and I stood above the Chinon moat, having seen Joan's bedroom, and the prison that held Eleanor of Aquitaine, it was a wintry, blustery day. There were few tourists around, fewer cars, and it was remarkably easy to imagine life five hundred years ago. It was not hard to picture oneself in armor, another Richard the Lion-Heart, fighting against Moslem infidels (something I've always wanted to do) and for the survival of civilization. Except in my case, of course, it would be Pete the Cat-Heart.

I let Norton out of his sack for a while and, after he sniffed through the ruins to his satisfaction, the three of us sat in the mostly crumbled courtyard, shivering slightly while we all pictured the past.

The present wasn't too terrible, either. We had a wonderful dinner that night at the Château de Marcay, near Chinon. The hotel is actually a fifteenth-century fortress, surrounded by its own vineyards, with forty rooms which are filled with antiques as well as whirlpools. There, they looked askance when I asked for a bowl of water for Norton—and insisted on bringing him milk instead—and looked absolutely horrified when I ordered the wine I wanted. The *sommelier,* a woman, which is rare over there, quietly and tactfully shook her head and offered to suggest something we might prefer. Although neither Janis nor I are ignoramuses about wine, we put ourselves in her superior hands and we were not disappointed. She brought us perhaps the most delicious white wine I've ever sipped, an Anjou, a Château d'Epire, produced by a M. et Mme. Bizard. I've never seen it before or since, but the taste will stay with me for the rest of my life. Of course, it didn't hurt that we were sipping it on giant oak chairs in front of a roaring, twenty-foot-wide hearth. My guess is that the atmosphere will help Norton remember the taste of that milk, too, a Château Borden, produced by Mme. Elsie.

The local Chinon wine was quite delectable as well, as we discovered the next day (and, if you go there, try the red, which is rarely imported to America—it's superb). We also discovered that small towns in America are not the only places that tend to be rather . . . uh . . . shall we say, rinky-dink.

Picture going to San Antonio to see the Alamo. As soon as you get within thirty miles, you start seeing The Alamo Motel, The Alamo Diner, The Alamo Bar & Grill, and The Alamo Fertilizer & Seed Shop. Everywhere you look, you see nothing but people using the name Alamo to promote something that has about as much to do with Davy Crockett and Jim Bowie as it does with life on Neptune. It's the same thing in the Loire Valley, although most of the touristy come-ons are somewhat more attractive than anything found in San Antonio. When you spend the night in the lovely villages of Loches or Ambois or Blois, every sign in town says something along the lines of CAFÉ LOUIS XIV or BOULANGERIE HENRI VIII or BLANCHERIE HENRI II (Henry the Second's Cleaners—it doesn't have quite the same ring in English, does it?).

One thing in the Loire that absolutely cannot be ruined by commercial greed is the wondrous *château* at Chenonceaux, built on top of a five-arched bridge over the river Cher.

I was first at Chenonceau (And so you don't think I'm a careless speller, please note that the French, typically, spell the town Chenonceau*x,* but the actual *château* is spelled Chenonceau. What can I say? That's why they're French.) in the summer of 1976, when I was young and hippieish. The place was crawling with tourists and it was brutally hot, but it was so wonderful it didn't matter. I was with David, my partner (yes, we go back that far together, although we didn't know what we were doing back then when it came to writing scripts), and our respective girlfriends (we didn't know what we were doing with them, either, but they're long gone from our lives), and we took rowboats on the river, rowing right under the castle as the sun was setting, then we sat in the middle of the Chenonceau grounds, amidst the alley of plane trees, drank wine and watched the incredible *son et lumière* show explaining the history of the castle.

Years later, when Janis, Norton, and I made our pilgrimage, there were no rowboats and no sound and light show and practically no tourists. It was cold and windy and, if possible, even more perfect than that summer day of long ago. As we toured the castle, nearly by ourselves, all the fireplaces had crackling fires in them. Looking through the windows, it was as if we were looking back into a glorious yet sobering past. We could palpably feel the plagues, the beheadings, the treachery, the splendor, the royalty that had all passed through the stone walls. None of the guards questioned that we were bringing a cat to study the Flemish tapestries, the four-poster beds, the Renaissance furniture, and the mind-boggling underground kitchen. I suppose with all that treachery and all those plagues, a Scottish Fold was no big deal.

Our last stop in the Loire—we were now getting eager to reach Provence—was in the lovely wine village of Sancerre.

This town has always had a fascination for me. When I was twenty-five, I had a novel published, called *The Dandy*, in which the lead character moves to France and chooses the town of Sancerre as his home because it produces his favorite white wine. Years later, the town—and the wine—didn't let me down. We wandered through the old part of the city, parts of which go back to the eleventh century, then we went a tastin'.

Sancerre happens to be Janis's favorite white wine, too, so we didn't hesitate to do as much sampling as we possibly could. And in this town, it's possible to do a *lot* of sampling. There must be over a hundred vineyards in a two- or three-mile area, each producing a wine more delicious than the last one. My favorite, and Janis's, was a small local *cave* right in town run by a father-and-son team. They were shut tight the day we were there, but a sign was posted saying that anyone who really wanted some wine should go three blocks further, make a right, then knock loudly at the door of the second house on the left. We followed the directions—a miracle in itself, nearly on a par with Jeanne d'Arc and the Dauphin—and found ourselves in someone's kitchen. The mother of the whole family, a rather chubby lady in her seventies, was making a huge vat of soup. We talked about their various wines while she stirred; then we sipped some different vintages while she stirred. We kept talking and sipping, she kept stirring, and finally we bought several cases to stick in the trunk of our car. I don't think she ever let go of her spoon the entire time.

Norton's favorite vineyard, however, was called the Cave Fouassier, right outside of town on the Route de Bourges. Norton didn't actually taste the wine, but he was very impressed with the vintner's dog, who, when he wanted to go out, would stand up on his two hind legs, put his two front paws on the doorknob, turn the knob, open the door, and scamper outside. It took us so long to taste and decide what to buy that by the time we were ready to leave, the dog wanted to come back in. So he went back on his hind legs, grabbed the doorknob with his front paws, and in he came.

It takes a lot to make Norton feel insecure. But I could tell from his expression that he was a bit awed by this feat.

"Hey," I told him, "practice makes perfect. It'll give you something to work on while we're here."

"You're talking to your cat again," Janis told me.

Norton didn't tell either one of us anything. He just stuck his head down inside his shoulder bag and thought about what he'd seen and what he was going to do about it.

We loaded our wine into the back of the car—there was now barely room to even put gas in—found the big highway, the *péage,* on our map, and, satiated with history, beauty, spirits, and genius dogs, sped on down to our new home.

a cat in provence

The house was perfect. And so was our new hometown.

The photographs we'd seen, convincing as they'd been, hadn't done either of them justice. The house was indeed three hundred years old. It was tucked away in a tiny side street (since the whole town was basically one street long, it wasn't difficult for the side streets to be tiny), the facade for the front was a pinkish, rough stucco, and the back was all the original stone. Downstairs was a small living room (very comfortably furnished), an eat-in kitchen with a fireplace (and no pancake flipper), a small *toilette,* and a separate bathroom with a tub and shower. On the second floor (which, mysteriously, the French call the first floor) were three bedrooms—one quite large, two smaller ones which formed a kind of mini-suite—another *toilette,* and another bathroom with tub. On the third floor (which the French call the second floor—if you think *you're* confused, try having a conversation with a French person about finding

103

something on one of these floors!) was a large, sprawling
office, sparsely furnished with a few chairs and a long, glass
desk, and then another bedroom, large with its own sink
tucked off to the side. There were also closets and cupboards everywhere you looked, all of which were filled with
Provençalian napkins and tablecloths and linens and towels,
as well as china and such essentials as an iron, a vacuum
cleaner, and lightbulbs. The furniture was old and comfortable and inviting; the kitchen was splendidly equipped. Best
of all, for my taste, was the sprawling *cave* underneath the
house. Using an old turnkey to open the thick wooden door
from the street, you then stepped into a stone dungeon. In
addition to such modern essentials as a washer/dryer and
a boiler, the *cave* was the place to stack the winter's supply
of wood and preserved jellies and jams. It also had a wine
cellar, protected by an iron gate, which needed another old
turnkey in order to pass through. Every time I went into the
wine cellar, I was positive some forty-pound guy with long
white hair was going to spring out at me and beg me to put
in a kind word with the captain of the king's guard.

All in all, this house was made for me.

More important, Norton took to it immediately.

Before we did anything else, I showed him the plump
couch and two easy chairs in the living room, explaining to
him that this was not our furniture and that he was not
allowed to scratch it. Ever. Janis, as usual, thought that I'd
lost my mind and that these complicated instructions probably would not penetrate the mind of a cat, but I do have to
say—and feel free to call our landlady anytime to verify
this—at the end of our year there, not a chair or a couch in
that house had so much as one scratch on it.

As soon as the rules were laid down, Norton went exploring. He sniffed around the living room and immediately

discovered his favorite exit from the house. The old-fashioned windows that swung open, looked over the backyard—and the entire Lubéron valley as well. A roof extended from right below the window, which functioned as an overhang for a patio. Norton immediately hopped up onto the window ledge, looked plaintively back in my direction until I figured out how to swing the window open (something I learned to do smoothly just about the time our year was up), then he hopped out onto the roof, stretched leisurely, lay down directly in the middle of a ray of sun, and began his life as a Provençal cat. All he needed was a beret and a baguette and I guarantee people would have come up to him and started to ask him what life was like in the *résistance.*

Another window swung open over the kitchen table, and Norton liked hopping out that one, too. He was also happy with the placement of his litter box, on the stone floor right by the back door. It became fairly standard procedure, during our time there, for Norton to pay a visit to his litter box, then immediately stand by the back door, waiting to be let out. Once out, he'd jump up onto the stone wall that ran up alongside the back steps to the house, assume a sphinxlike position, and spend as much time there as direct sunlight allowed.

The garden was a cat's delight (as well as Janis's greatest pleasure, since there is nothing that gives her as much pure joy as sticking her hands in dirt and either planting a beloved perennial or ripping out some dreaded weed). Our Provençal garden was roughly the size of a football field, divided up into four distinct square levels and sections, each square separated by an ancient stone wall. Directly out the back door, the first square had an enormous spruce tree in the middle of it, and next to that, a small fig tree. Around

the perimiters were roses, pansies, tulips, wisteria, and lots
and lots of herbs—including huge hedges of rosemary. Up
against the house, an extension, really, of this part of the
garden, was a stone patio, set up with several chairs and a
small dining table. The weather was so beautiful that we ate
outside almost every day until mid-December.

If you made a right turn out the back door, took ten
paces, and then went down a couple of stone steps, you'd
reach the second square of the garden. This one was dominated by a large lavender garden; the well-defined rectan-
gle of lavender was probably twelve feet wide and fifteen
feet long. Past the lavender, and running along the boundary of the property, was another patio, also set up with a
small table and chairs. Built into the wall there was a stone
barbecue, complete with grill.

Facing straight ahead, still standing on the right side of
the yard, you could go down a couple of stone steps to the
third quarter of the garden. This one was dominated by a
luscious cherry tree and a round stone table, the perfect
place to sit and sip a late-afternoon *kir.*

To the left, and down six or seven more steps, was the
last part of the garden, this one fairly sparse. An olive tree
sat toward the right of the space, as did a bay laurel tree,
and the left boundary was lined with raspberry bushes (we
were eating ripe, delicious raspberries for breakfast until
the first week in December).

Norton spent hours and hours exploring every nook and
cranny of this garden. He loved it out there. For one thing,
there were no mean mockingbirds to torment him, as there
were in Sag Harbor, only a bunch of fairly pleasant black
and white magpies. Plus, I'm sure the mice were particularly delicious, since they had been fattened up on camem-
bert and roquefort since birth.

As much as we adored the house—and we gradually added our personal touches to it: the occasional quilt here, a piece of rough hewn pottery there—the town in which we now resided was even more special.

Goult truly is a village touched by magic. It is as lovely as any of the small towns in the entire region yet has escaped any trappings of tourism, managing to remain completely unspoiled. It's small, approximately eleven hundred people, has a thousand-year-old castle, and is nicknamed "Le Village Caché" ("the hidden village") according to local legend because it's tucked away on top of a hill and seems to disappear, à la Brigadoon, when one is trying to spot it from the road down below. Up until the spring of '92, there was only one restaurant in town; now there are two. Up until that same time, there was one *épicerie* in town; now there are two. There have always been two butchers, though I can't fathom how a town of a eleven hundred people supports two butchers, especially since—and this could only be in France—they are right next door to each other, keep the exact same hours, and are closed the exact same day of the week.

We—the three of us, with Norton lagging behind and periodically disappearing into strange alleys and *caves,* including someone's garage, which turned out to have once been the town's ancient olive oil mill—toured the town and oriented ourselves, once we explored the various rooms and gardens of the house. Satisfied that we'd done well—having no idea yet quite *how* well we'd done—we returned to the house to begin the process of making it our home. The first step was to unpack the various boxes we'd sent on ahead (yes, yes, we had even *more* stuff than the millions of pounds we lugged in our suitcases). There was only one problem: There *were* no boxes.

This brings us to an important rule of thumb that one must understand before ever moving to France: When it comes to anything involving rules, regulations, and laws, absolutely nothing in the country makes any sense whatsoever.

A case in point:

Since I was neither retired nor wealthy, and since my cat was expecting to be kept in the style to which he'd become accustomed, I had to do some work while we were in France. As this is the twentieth century, I needed a computer, a fax machine, and a telephone answering machine to do that work. And thus the nightmare began.

My first mistake was shipping those key items over instead of packing them away and carrying them (this was important because in all the trips we made in and out of the Marseille airport, we never even *saw* a customs official, much less one who would rummage through a suitcase). My second mistake was being honest. On the UPS form, right below the line where they promise you'll receive your goods in two days, is a blank space where you're supposed to list exactly what it is you're shipping. On my form, kook that I was, I put exactly that: a fax machine, a laptop computer, a telephone answering machine, three electrical transformers (which weigh twenty pounds apiece, cost eighty dollars apiece, and are an absolute necessity for any American spending time in France), and some sweaters (which, along with bubble wrap, were used to cushion all the machinery so they wouldn't be smashed into little bits). UPS couldn't have been nicer or more efficient and they weren't even that expensive. All my stuff even arrived in Paris exactly on time. And when it arrived, I got a call from someone named Monsieur Kebé at French Customs. We had a very pleasant chat—although Monsieur Kebé spoke no English and, at this point, my French sounded a lot like Inspector Clouseau; I was basically speaking English with a French accent and hoping that would pass—until I was told that it was impossible to allow my cartons into the country. It seems that the French phone company, which is government-owned, has a monopoly on phone machines *(répondeurs)* and fax machines. So no such machines are allowed to be brought in. Ever. Never.

I was told that no amount of money, no amount of pleading, no amount of *anything* would ever convince them to let me bring these machines into France. It was impossible. Out of the question. End of story. *Tout est dit!*

I did some checking. There really did seem to be a law against bringing in phone machines. The government made everyone buy only French phone equipment. As near as I could tell, however, there were no exact laws against bringing in computers—they're not owned by the phone company, thank god!—but it seems the French just don't really *like* it when one is brought in. They prefer you buy one of their own *ordinateurs*. As far as the sweaters were concerned, they were a little concerned that I'd be opening a sweater store, which would be illegal for an American, so they thought they'd keep those, too.

I'll skip most of the unpleasantries. Like anything else in France, what was needed most here was neither money to bribe nor logic to convince. What was needed was patience. And a French friend named Nicholas who lived in Paris and went to see Monsieur Kebé in person. After three days of conversation, Nicholas called me to say that he explained to Monsieur Kebé that I was a writer and a publisher and that these machines were not to be sold in France but were the tools of my trade. Ah! Although it was still out of the question—absolutely and finally—Monsieur K wanted me to fax him my passport, a letter from my French publisher, and a copy of the jacket of my latest book. I was happy to do that, I explained—except that Monsieur Kebé had my fax machine. That was why we were having this conversation in the first place!

They acknowledged a certain logic on my part, but none-theless they wanted what they wanted. I found a public fax in the nearby town of Murs and was able to send them what they'd asked for. It only took me six hours, which means I could have taken the TGV up to Paris, dropped the material off, and trained it on back home in the same amount of time it took me to fax something. The reason it took so much time was also fairly typical Provence (and fairly typical me). Janis decided to stay home to begin work in the garden. So Norton and I got in our car and went exploring. First we went to the town of Apt, the largest nearby town. After asking in the bookstore, a café, and a pottery store, I found out that there was no public fax in Apt. The nearest one was in Murs, a town of perhaps seven hundred people. No problem. We headed off to Murs and got to the *mairie,* the town hall, just a few minutes after noon. Which was a few minutes too late because the *mairie* was closed until three. No problem. I was in France; I could adapt to a different speed and lifestyle. I'd simply go to a café in Murs, have a little wine, read a little bit, pet my cat, and wait for three o'clock to arrive. Except that Murs didn't *have* a café. It was too small. So Norton and I drove back to Apt, where we found a café and a carafe of chilled rosé wine. Two hours later, it was back to Murs. But there was some sort of emergency and the *mairie* still wasn't open. (Later, I think I pieced together the emergency: The woman who worked at the *mairie* had a daughter who'd had a fight with her husband. I couldn't understand what they fought over, though I think it had something to do with a beef stew the daughter either had or hadn't made for that night's dinner.) At 3:45 the woman arrived and, apologetically, opened up the town hall. She reminded me of Jo Van Fleet in *Cool Hand Luke,* wheezing and creaking and coughing while she talked. We climbed the two flights of stairs together, then, exhausted, she had to rest for a few minutes before we could get on to business. I showed her my passport and the other things I'd brought and asked her if I could use the town's fax machine. *Of course,* she told me. *Absolutely no problem. Fine,* I told her. *Well, maybe there's* one *little problem,* she said. Then she told me she didn't know how to work the fax machine. No one had ever asked to use it before. So we had to wait for her coworker, a man of sixty years or so, to come huffing and puffing up the stairs, too, to try to send the material. He was the French William Demarest, grumpy, mumbling constantly, very concerned about everything, and extremely tan and leathery.

An hour later, we'd all basically figured the sucker out. Sure enough, when I tried faxing everything through, it worked. (Although when the first sheet of paper passed through, both William Demarest and Jo Van Fleet did double takes. "What eez zat noise?" she asked. "I think it's the fax being transmitted," I told her. She looked at him for confirmation and he just shrugged; now that it was working, he'd washed his hands of the whole matter.)

I then asked how much I owed—and this was a major stumper. She had no idea, so she paced for a while, pursed her lips in that French way, shook her head, and muttered to herself. She tried asking Bill Demarest, but he could only make puffing noises with his mouth and slowly shake his head back and forth. I just let them talk and pace and puff, and at some point they settled on twenty francs, about four dollars.

On Day 5 of the Fax/Computer Hostage Situation, customs told me I should forget about what they'd said earlier: I could have all my things after all—for a mere fifteen hundred dollars in import tax. Outraged, I told them to ship it all back to America. I'd rather buy new equipment, I said. (A mistake: A French phone machine, even a crummy one, costs four hundred dollars. A fax machine goes for about fifteen hundred. Don't even *think* about buying a computer there. Anything electric costs two to three times as much as it costs in the USA.) Luckily, however, they paid no attention to me. French people hardly ever pay attention to anything stupid we foreigners say.

Day 10: They asked me to send them a copy of *The Cat Who Went to Paris.*

Day 14: Monsieur Kebé liked the book. I decided he's more suited to be a literary critic for *The New York Times* than a French Customs official. He also says I can have my equipment for a mere thousand dollars. I get angry but, keeping his superb literary taste in mind, I don't go berserk.

Day 17: My friend Nicholas calls me to say I'm getting everything—for free. No problem whatsoever; it'll all arrive within two days. He said the final conversation in the customs room between Monsieur Kebé and his superior went as follows:

"Hmmm, he really seems to be a writer."

"What should we do?"

"Hmmmm. More wine?"

"Thank you. Do you think he's importing these things to sell them here?"

"No, do you?"

"I don't know. I don't think he could get very much for those sweaters."

"Oh, let's send the stuff to him. It takes up a lot of room here."

"It certainly does. Okay, let's send it. Could I have a drop more of the white?"

~~~

Once my home office was set up, I could relax, rather than spend most of the day pacing around the town of Goult muttering about the end of my career. This final settling in also meant that our family of three could develop a routine. (Although here are two hints to help you relax a bit more if you're American and you ever set up a home office in France. Hint #1: Bring a spare phone machine because you will definitely blow up the first one trying to figure out how to hook it up to the transformer without blowing it up on the different current. Hint #2: After you finish ripping your hair out of your head because you can't figure out how to plug an American phone into a French phone jack, go to a French hardware or electrical appliance store. They have special plugs that fit American phones—even though they're not supposed to, because, as we all remember, it's illegal to have an American phone. Don't ask questions, just get one.)

Our routine was a fairly relaxed one, since the purpose of this whole trip was to exchange our insanely hectic New York lifestyle for one that made some philosophical, psychological, and emotional sense (and, since we were in France, we figured we also had to eat and drink as much as we possibly could). I would get up, have my early-morning two-mile run through the vast expanse of vineyards, then, huffing and puffing on my way back up the hill to Goult, I'd stop off at the patisserie in Lumiere, the town closest to us, for a baguette or a couple of croissants. By the time I'd get to the house, Janis would have made coffee. We'd have our breakfast—bread, honey, jam, and coffee—together, on Elisabeth's china and in her giant, soup-sized bowls; sometimes Norton would join us, sometimes he'd already be perched on the roof or the wall outside. Then I'd go upstairs to work for the morning while Janis would garden or go off to a museum or just study her French. Come lunchtime, we'd rendezvous, deciding, depending on our mood, whether to have a luxurious and extravagant lunch, or a quick peasant lunch at a *routier* (truckstop) followed by a two- or three-hour session exploring the region. If I didn't have to work in the afternoon (I was busy working for Random House as well as writing a screenplay and a book; I know that doesn't sound like much of a vacation, but believe me, after running a company and producing a TV series and writing a book all at the same time, working two jobs on my own time was the equivalent of lying on the beach in the Caribbean), we could explore further. For dinner, we'd either hit a local restaurant or expand our culinary abilities (not to brag, but we both became fairly proficient in the kitchen while we were there) or, as our circle of friends expanded, hope that one of our new pals would invite us over for an *aïoli* or a *maigret de canard*.

Norton's routine became fairly standardized also, once we worked out his sleeping arrangements. For the first couple of weeks we were there, we had a tiny bed and he was too outraged at the lack of space to sleep with us. There was barely room for the two humans to get through the night without tumbling onto the floor, though of course this didn't stop me from trying to squeeze Norton in. But he would have none of it. Needless to say, this didn't sit well with me; I do not sleep well unless my cat is within hugging distance at almost all times. So I was delighted when our landlady agreed to buy the house a new and much larger bed, although, like everything else, having a bed delivered in France is not like having a bed delivered anywhere else. More than anything in the world, French people love to talk. It doesn't matter if the tone is argumentative, questioning, sympathetic, informational, or philosophical, as long as talk is involved. So the first thing was that the guys from the furniture store came over to take a look at the house—and talk about it. They examined the front door to make sure the bed would fit. That was good for a five-minute chat. Then they examined the hallway. That seemed worth talking about for ten minutes or so. They examined the curved stone stairway that led up to our bedroom. That was a particularly interesting topic of conversation. How old was the stairway? Was it original? How many steps were there? How steep was it? Did I ever slip and fall down it in the middle of the night?

They managed to examine the bedroom—as well as the three other bedrooms in the house, just in case the bed wouldn't fit in the room for which it was intended. Then they discussed the door and the hallway and the various bedrooms some more. After forty-five minutes of this, I suggested that perhaps it might work best if they actually measured the doorways and the width of the stairs. Yes, they agreed. That was a very good idea. Did I happen to have a tape measure? I did happen to have one, and after another forty-five minutes during which we discussed the furniture in the house, the weather, the advantages and disadvantages of Goult, a date on which they could deliver the bed, and, finally, drank a couple of cups of coffee, they left. A week later, when the bed came, the problem with

Norton was solved. He had enough room to be comfortable and went right back to his usual spot of sleeping near
my neck and chest.

The first night of the new bed, we went to the local
restaurant in Goult, Le Tunneau, owned by a charming guy
and good chef, Patrick, to celebrate. It was Norton's first
time at Le Tunneau and he was served a little duck by way
of introduction. He was accepted as just another customer.
There was no fuss whatsoever, even from the dog dining
there that night. During the course of the meal, Norton
wandered a little bit (the restaurant is a converted *cave,* so
there were plenty of interesting sniffing and scratching
places). Every so often, he would hop back up on his seat
and help himself to a taste of my rabbit or Janis's chicken.
After dinner, stuffed and quite content, the three of us
headed home and went to sleep. Janis woke up in the middle of the night to the following picture: I was sound asleep
on the left side of the bed; she was lying on the right side.
Stretched out exactly in the middle, head on both of our
pillows, body under the blanket, was our Scottish Fold,
sound asleep yet purring so loudly he'd woken her up.

Once the sleep routine was settled, Norton's day was not
so different from our own. After a fine French breakfast
(canned rabbit was the clear winner as far as he was concerned), he would sun himself outside in one of his three
or four favorite spots. He would, as often as not, come out
to lunch with us and explore whenever it was appropriate.
Depending on how hard we'd judged his day, he'd either
dine out with us or stay home like a normal cat, content to
eat more canned rabbit and then fall asleep.

Norton had never been a particularly social animal, not
when it came to other four-legged creatures. He was not
around a lot of cats in New York (he'd been in one fight—

recounted in extraordinary dramatic detail in the *very* underrated yet moving and puckish *The Cat Who Went to Paris*—which did not end happily or with much of Norton's dignity remaining) and his exposure to dogs, while harmless and uneventful, had also been infrequent. That all changed in Provence.

At my last count, there were forty-two million cats in Goult, give or take a million. They were all over the place, everywhere and anywhere you turned. None of them, it seemed, had a home, although every person in town knew every one of the cats, usually by name. Our landlady, Elisabeth, was a longtime cat lover and, even though she didn't have any of her own, she used to leave food out for *tous les chats Goultois*. Which meant that we usually had several cats strolling the property in search of nourishment.

I don't know whether it was the fact that Norton felt, as an expatriot cat, that he was intruding on the Goult cats' turf, but he was far friendlier and more relaxed around these fellows than he ever was with the felines in Sag Harbor or Fire Island. There was the occasional hiss and unmistakable cat-fight screech, and every so often he'd try to act like a tough guy (usually when he was safely inside and knew all doors and windows to the garden were closed), but on the whole, Norton seemed to accept the French *que será, será* way of life and actually made a few pals.

One of his closer friends was a solid black cat, whose name we learned was Othello. We never learned who Othello's owner was, but Othello's demeanor was befitting of his regal name; he used to preen all around the town, though his special spot was a bench that was placed in a small grass triangle—a *very* tiny public park—from which he liked to survey the townspeople's comings and goings.

I don't think Norton and Othello used to go to soccer

matches together or exchange Christmas presents, but there was a certain amount of male bonding that went on. I do know that one day, as I was strolling to one of the village butchers, I did see Norton and Othello together sitting outside the café. Don't worry: They weren't being served. At least, not when I passed by.

Probably the funniest animal in town was a bulldog named Archie (pronounced Ar-*shee*). Archie was as solid as bulldogs usually are and he was a dead ringer for the older J. Edgar Hoover, except I never saw Archie wearing a dress. Archie's owner was a young woman who would often walk him through town on a leash, but just as often, we'd find Archie hanging out around our front door, leashless and ownerless. Everyone in town knew Archie (I think he must have, at one point or another, drooled several kilos of saliva on every person in Goult), but he handled his celebrity status quite well. He was always friendly, to humans and to Scottish Fold cats. After several weeks of eyeing each other warily, Norton and Archie achieved a certain comfort level. When in each other's presence, Archie would do his best not to snort and breathe so heavily that he scared Norton, and Norton eventually got to the point where he would stroll within inches of the bulldog without having to sprint, hiss, or make all his fur stand up on end.

I know everyone likes a happy ending, but I'm sorry to say that Norton never did come to grips with those little, friendly birds who were in the outdoor cage a couple of blocks from our house. After his wimpy run-in with them, which I mentioned earlier, he stayed as far away from that part of town as he possibly could.

Norton got to be pals—or at least nodding acquaintances—with several animals outside of Goult, too.

One of our favorite restaurants, a breathtakingly charming place up in the mountains, the Auberge de la Loube, in the town of Buoux, was wonderful not only because of the owners/chefs but because of the cats and dogs who populated the place.

The restaurant is a four-hundred-year-old stone farmhouse, quite small, maybe twelve tables, dominated by an enormous fireplace and decorated with all sorts of horse accoutrements—everything from photos to bridles to reins to saddles. The owner, Maurice, is a terrific guy, quite friendly and elegant, a little bemused at how successful his country inn has become since Peter Mayle rhapsodized about him in *A Year in Provence*. (The reason there's so much horse memorabilia around is that Maurice restores antique carriages—as in horse and carriages. Some of them are nineteenth-century American carriages, most are French, all are exquisite. When the weather's nice, it's possible to arrange for a carriage ride in the mountains and a picnic lunch or dinner. One other thing about the Auberge de la Loube: For months, we assumed "Loube" was some variation on the Lubéron valley and mountain range, of which Buoux is a part. However, we asked Maurice one night and he explained to us that—and remember, I warned you about this earlier—*loube* is, in fact, Provençal for "wolf.") His wife, whom we knew only as Madame Maurice, is equally terrific, and she took particular pleasure in Norton's visits to the Auberge.

Maurice and his wife have three dogs, a gorgeous Irish setter, a black lab, and some kind of very friendly mutt, as well as a big, fat, easygoing orange cat. The dogs roam the two rooms of the restaurant, camping under the table of whoever looks most likely to drop food on the floor, either unintentionally or out of pity for the tortured, starving look the dogs can assume at a moment's notice. All three of the

canines also spend a lot of time burrowed in the two hol-
lows that are dug into the stone underneath the huge
hearth. The cat, naturally, is much more dignified. He
strolls around the restaurant, quite haughtily, until he finds
a willing sucker, then he jumps up into his or her lap and
settles in for the night (or until Madame Maurice spots him
and swats him away, yelling at him to leave the customers
alone). The dogs and cat get along famously, and they all
switch back and forth effortlessly from being outdoor to
indoor animals. There is a famous local story about the Irish
setter, who tends to roam more than the others. He was
spotted one day in the town of Apt, which is a good seven
or eight miles away from the Auberge. When he was recognized, as he was walking confidently through the town,
some concerned friend convinced him to hop into his truck
and brought him back to the Auberge, where they suspect
he makes such lengthy sojourns on a regular basis.

The first time we brought Norton up to meet the gang
at the Auberge, he was greeted warmly by all concerned
and fit in as if he'd been born to the French mountain life.
He had quite a few dinners up there, and humans, dogs, and
cat were always glad to see him. When the restaurant wasn't
crowded, he'd be allowed his own chair. When it was
crowded—which was more often than not—he'd either sit
on my lap or find a nice spot on the table in which to settle
in. If we got a window seat, he was also more than happy
to dine in comfort on the stone window ledge.

The food at Auberge de la Loube is a cat's delight, as well
as the delight of any sane person, because it's delicious and
completely satisfying. They also do something that's common in France, which is take the pressure off the diner as
far as having to choose is concerned; basically, they order
for you. When you sit down at Auberge de la Loube, an

enormous tray of Provençal appetizers is placed before you. On the tray are small dishes, filled with local delicacies. A typical sampling will include onion marmalade, tiny quail's eggs, the best *tapenade* ever made, candied carrots, rabbit pâté, a very garlicy yogurt, *anchois* and pickled cucumbers. All to be eaten with a basketful of French bread, which is sliced before your eyes with an antique bread cutter which resembles nothing so much as the guillotine that sliced off the head of Marie Antoinette and probably a whole bunch of other cake-eaters.

Once sated, you're left only with having to make choices from the good, inexpensive, and mostly local wine list and four or five options for a main course. In the fall and winter, the possibilities range from *sanglier,* which is wild boar (often served in a stew, with a thick, very dark sauce, called a *civet*), rabbit (sometimes served in the same kind of stew, sometimes served roasted), stuffed or roast veal, and occasionally a fish, usually salmon or *lotte*. In the spring and summer, the choices are usually the same base foods, although prepared in a somewhat lighter fashion. Oddly enough, restaurants in Provence rarely serve chicken, as that's perceived, historically, as poor people's food.

Perhaps it has occurred to you already, but when one lives in the south of France, one becomes totally obsessed with food. We would get calls from friends back in America wondering whether we'd lost our minds because they'd just received a three-page letter from one of us which was about nothing but one luscious and delicious tomato we'd bought at the market. It reached the point where people were expecting daily faxes from us to find out what we'd eaten for dinner the night before.

It didn't take long for each of us—me, Janis, and Norton—to grab hold of this obsession and refuse to let go.

After we'd been there several months, we had the ultimate compliment paid to us by an elderly French woman, who prepared us dinner one night. As we were eating her succulent lamb, we were discussing other great meals we'd had since we'd been in Europe. We're munching on her roast potatoes talking about a pasta dish we'd eaten in Tuscany; we're scarfing down her white beans in *vinaigre* while extolling the virtues of a bouillabaise we'd had in Marseille; we're moaning over her *tarte aux pommes* but manage to get in a few highly charged words about a raspberry beignet we'd stumbled upon at an open-air market. Finally she says, in a throaty voice with just a touch of a French accent, "Congratulations. You are now truly French. To eat a fine meal and do nothing but talk about other foods means you're now one of us."

Hey, when in Rome (or Provence), you know what I mean?

Our days began to revolve around food.

One of the great thrills of living there is to shop at the open-air markets, which move from town to town, depending on the day of the week. When we finally figured out the schedule, we began to move along with them. Tuesday was a small market in the village of Gordes. Saturday was Apt. Both towns were convenient to Goult, so we became Tuesday and Saturday regulars. The biggest and most spectacular market was on Sunday, in the town of L'isle-sur-la-Sorgue. There the appeal was not just food but miles of stalls filled with splendid antiques. Going to market on Sunday became, to me, the equivalent of a five-year-old kid going to Disneyland.

L'isle-sur-la-Sorgue is not a large town—perhaps three thousand people—but on Sunday mornings it quadruples in size. The village itself is quite beautiful. It's flat, unlike most of the towns around it, which are perched on hilltops, and has winding cobblestone streets lurching in every direction. It's also built on a series of canals, which surround the town and, thanks to the clear, rushing water and the waterwheels and the wooden bridges, give it much of its atmosphere. During the week (except Thursday, when there's a mini-version of the big market), the place is subdued, quiet, and charming. But on Sundays, from seven in the morning until one o'clock in the afternoon, it's a madhouse. Every inch of the cobblestone streets is packed with vendors and shoppers. The vendors have staked out their particular territories over a period of years (in some cases, I'm fairly sure that certain families have been selling their wine or their potatoes in the same spot for about three *hundred* years or so); the shoppers mill aimlessly until they see what they want or, especially as the seasons get warmer and more tourists show up, shove their way through the crowds to try to get the best of everything. It's so European it can make you cry with pleasure, especially when the local organ grinder, who happens to look like a young Maurice Chevalier, strolls through the crowded market in feathered cap and glowing cape belting out his romantic ballads.

Norton quite liked being lugged through the L'isle market in his shoulder bag. If he played his cards right, which he usually did, he could come away with little bits of everything from homemade sausage to strong, smelly goat cheese to chocolate tarts. Janis and I also usually played our cards right. It didn't take us long to find our favorite vendors and become regular buyers (many of the same vendors also went to the Gordes and the Apt markets, so we'd see them two or three times a week). One of our favorites was a small, wonderfully nice and cheery man who made mouth-watering tarts and sold them from his truck, with the aid of

his eight-year-old daughter. He baked in the town of Ve-
nasque, about forty-five minutes away, via a curving, mountain road, and then carried his scrumptious works of art to
the marketplaces. His artichoke tart was like nectar of the
gods, as was his *poireaux* (leeks) creation, but his shallot tart
was his masterpiece, as delicious as anything I've ever tasted
that wasn't covered with chocolate. And while we're on the
subject, he happened to make a chocolate and caramel tart
that, in my humble opinion, belongs in the Louvre. Luckily
for everyone's cholesterol count, we figured there couldn't
possibly be more than seven or eight pounds of butter in it.

In addition to our tart guy (that's the way we started
thinking of him: Our Tart Guy), there was a Cambodian
man who made the most delicious *poulet rôti* that was ever
*rôti*ed. He was a lawyer in Cambodia but wasn't allowed to
take the French bar (or whatever the equivalent of the bar
is in France) and so made perfect roast chickens instead.
There was a young Algerian who aggressively sold vats of
incredible *tapenade* and *anchois* (crushed olive paste and
crushed anchovies). There was also an old, cronelike
woman who was missing at least two-thirds of her teeth and
who sold goat cheese so strong you could barely stand up
after a small taste. She sold them in little heart-shaped
cheeses, each one flavored with rosemary or garlic or shal-
lots or—and this one I'm guessing on but I think I'm
close—really old socks. We bought cheese from her every
week and her products became a benchmark for any and all
of our visitors. It was simple: Someone would arrive from
New York, exhausted from the long flight and drive from
Marseille. We'd sit him, her, or them down, set up a glass
of wine from a nearby *cave,* and place a plate of the crone's
goat cheese before them. If they tasted it, and then hungrily
dug in for more, appreciating the earthiness and power, we

knew we were in for a good visit. If, on the other hand, the
guest or guests got a slice of the garlic cheese halfway down
their throat, then started gasping and calling either for
water or a gun with which to shoot themselves, we knew
that we'd have trouble sharing our Provençal tastes and
pleasures.

Norton, in the meantime, was developing his own very
particular tastes and pleasures when it came to French food.

With all our travels, prior to and including this year
abroad, Norton seemed to prefer French cat food to any
other. His favorites were Whiskas, Gourmet, and the
French Friskies. Gourmet was the cheaper brand, more of
a peasant cat food, but at times clearly satisfying to the cat
palate. The nice thing about Gourmet was that they sold it
in a handy three-pack *(le menu 3 étoiles; 3 boîtes de 195 grams)*.
They had many different flavors, most of which pleased my
cat. In the category of *Les Pavés Mignons,* they had your basic
Délice de Viandes, your fresh *Au Saumon,* and the ever-popu-
lar *Au Foie et Volaille.* In the category of *Best Supporting
Terrine,* they had an overload of delicacies: *Au Lapin et Foie*
(definitely in Norton's top three); *L'Agneau et Volaille*
(yummmmm), *Au Foie et Veau, Délice de Colin, Aux Trois
Volailles, Au Foie et Volaille* (a certain pattern does seem to
be emerging, though I'm not sure if Norton ever noticed
that there were the same basic ingredients, cleverly mixed
together in as many different combinations as those Gourmet folks could think up), *Au Boeuf et Rognons* (also quite
a favorite), *Panache de Poissons* (not a chance; Norton never
succumbed to this one), *Au Gibier* (Norton was quite fond
of this can; Janis would leave the room as soon as it was
opened—a *boîte* filled with all sort of giblets is not her idea
of culinary heaven), *Au Poulet et Rognons* (boring but a solid
choice), *Au Lapin et Foie* (now you're talking!), and just

before we left, Gourmet introduced the *nouveau* flavor of the year, *Au Rognons et Volaille* (bravo!). As if this weren't enough, they also had a category called *La Mousse,* which only had one flavor, but was nothing to sneer at, *Au Rognons et Volaille.*

Although Gourmet was not, in fact, the crème de la crème of French cat foods, I had a soft spot for them because of the Club Gourmet one could join. On specially marked cans of their food was an announcement: *Vous qui êtes passionnés de chats, rejoignez vite le CLUB GOURMET, un club spécialement crée pour vous: vous bénéficierez des privilèges d'un club prestigieux et des conseils châteaux de CATY.* Translated as best as I can manage, this means: You who are passionate about cats, quickly sign up for the Gourmet Club, a special club created for you: you benefit from the privileges of a prestigious club and the counsel of the cat castle.

Friskies wasn't bad, if you go by Norton's appetite, and they had the advantage of being slightly healthier. Well, okay, I wouldn't call it health food, but at least with their *Au Foie et Volaille,* they added *petits légumes.* After Norton munched on these, I didn't feel so bad about giving him a lick of my dessert.

Whoever was the creative force in the Whiskas kitchen was a fine *chef de cuisine,* also. Norton's favorite *boîte* on their list was the clever combo of *Au Lapin et à la Dinde* (rabbit and turkey; you've got to admit it sounds good). Whiskas also was thoughtful enough to tell you a little bit about their food on the back of each box top:

● *WHISKAS a préparé pour votre chat les "Petits Régals":*
● *des recettes richement elaborées avec de delicieux petits morceaux et une odeur appétissante*

- *une présentation soignée, en portion repas, facile à utiliser, avec un couvercle refermable*
- *Pour varier les plaisirs de votre chat, les "Petits Régals" vous proposent trois variétés raffinées: Au Bouef et aux Rognons, A la Volaille et au Foie, Au Lapin et à la Dinde.*

Words to bring comfort to any cat and cat owner:

- *WHISKAS has prepared for your cat the Little Meals:*
- *recipes richly elaborated with delicious little morsels and an appetizing odor*
- *a careful presentation, in meal-sized portions, easy to use with a recloseable top*
- *To vary the pleasures of your cat, the "Petits Régals" proposes to you three refined varieties: Beef and Kidney, Fowl and Liver, Rabbit and Turkey.*

Bon appétit.

At the beginning, it all seemed exotic and quaint and a little eccentric. The more time we spent there, however, the saner life in Provence became. What was happening, without our realizing it, was that we were becoming part of the community.

Though we'd only been gone a few months, America was receding into the distance. We didn't have a television in Goult—a deliberate choice, mostly Janis's I have to say, but a very wise one—which cut us off from a lot of our own culture. Our French, at this stage, was barely serviceable, but almost no one we were spending time with spoke any English, so we quickly got out of the habit of speaking the only language we could communicate with.

That left us in a strange though not unpleasant kind of limbo.

There were all sorts of things we had not anticipated before we moved from one country to another. Or if we had anticipated them, they didn't turn out quite the way we'd expected.

We knew we'd have to do something about money, which meant we'd have to figure out what to do about using a French bank. Cleverly (I thought), before we left New York, I'd spoken to someone at Crédit Lyonnais, the second largest bank in France. The person in their New York office told me that they did indeed have a branch fairly near Goult, in the town of Cavaillon.

Perfect.

After our arrival and two or three days of doing nothing but soaking in atmosphere, appreciating the local beauty, and screaming at the customs officials, we decided we had to do something practical, so we drove into Cavaillon and found Crédit Lyonnais.

It was easy. The very first street we turned down, once we hit town, had a bank on it with a big LYONNAISE sign. We parked in front of the bank and went inside. (Which was not very easy; the French have a strange system where you have to punch a buzzer to get in one door, then you're trapped in a tiny room before you can open the other door. The problem is in trying to open the second door, which can't be done until the first door is completely shut. Janis, Norton, and I spent a good ten minutes trapped in between doors, until some kindly soul in the bank finally started waving his hands and pointing and shouting and showed us how to get through.) Once inside, we were golden. The bank was very small, almost sleepy compared to most banks. In very simple French, I asked if anyone spoke English.

They told me that the manager, Monsieur Gilbert Rebattu, spoke a little English, and moments later we were ushered into Monsieur Rebattu's office.

When they say "a little English" in Provence, they mean a *little* English. Monsieur Rebattu, a slight man with a dark mustache and a somewhat nervous but absolutely charming manner, knew how to say "hello" and "good-bye" and practically nothing else in between. He was, however, extraordinarily nice and helpful, and spent almost an hour with us, helping us fill out the forms. (Normally, this would have been a five-minute meeting. But between my French and Monsieur Rebattu's English, we needed the hour.) He told us what type of banking would be best for us, he explained how we should write checks, he even explained the French banking system, which makes a lot more sense than the American system. In France, no one asks for I.D. when you write out a check. You don't have to show a driver's license or a credit card; it's exactly the same as handing over cash. Monsieur Rebattu explained that that was because people in France don't bounce checks. There is no system of credit there (one of the reasons that the country's not in debt for hundreds of billions of dollars, unlike other countries we might name). When a French person pays with a Visa card, that money is taken right out of his or her bank account. If a French person ever bounces a check, he loses all banking privileges for a year—which basically means he can't live. I think Monsieur Rebattu also said something about never again being able to drink wine or watch Jerry Lewis movies or eat *tarte tatin,* too, but, again, my French was still pretty rusty.

Once this was all explained to us, we put in enough money to ensure we'd never lose our banking privileges. We received our temporary checks right away—Monsieur

Rebattu had the good sense to ask if Norton would require his own checkbook; the answer was a definite no—and then we were all set. But as we thanked our new bank manager and stood up to leave, Monsieur Rebattu put his hand on my arm and said, in a very soft voice, "Excuse me, *monsieur.* But what is it that made you choose our bank?"

I explained that it was quite simple. We'd been told that Crédit Lyonnais was the most convenient place to bank because there were branches all over the country. We'd also been told that the Crédit Lyonnais in Cavaillon was the closest to our town. There was nothing more to it: the biggest, the best, the closest. *Voilà.*

Monsieur Rebattu nodded unhappily. The smile that had been on his face disappeared. He was not a physically imposing man to begin with and he seemed to shrink before our very eyes.

"Yes, I thought it was something like that," he sighed.

"Is there a problem?" I wanted to know. I didn't really want to know, but I sensed it was a question that had to be asked. I was right.

"This is *not* Crédit Lyonnais, *monsieur.*"

"It's not? But the sign out front . . ."

"This is Lyonnaise de Banque."

I looked at Janis. She looked at me. Norton refused to look at either one of us. "That's not the same thing?" I asked, trying my best not to look as miserable as I felt.

Monsieur Rebattu nodded knowingly and wistfully, then, looking much unhappier than I could possibly be, he shrugged and gently said, "It's not too late to change. I will understand."

By this time, Janis was practically in tears and half in love with Monsieur Rebattu for being so kind and thoughtful, so

we both shook our heads—after a moment's hesitation—
and boldly declared, "Absolutely not. Lyonnaise de Banque
is the bank for us!"

They didn't bring out a band or have a parade but it was
close. I don't know when they last had a new customer, but
clearly this was an event of the first order for the gang at
Lyonnaise de Banque. Monsieur Rebattu shook our hands
(and petted Norton) and thanked us profusely. Then he
proudly took us through the rest of the bank, which took
all of fourteen seconds, introducing us to all the other em-
ployees, who looked at us as if they couldn't comprehend
that we were actually putting money in their, shall we say,
"modest" place of business.

It turned out to be a great move. (Except for the time our
friend Norm came over from New York and wanted to
change American dollars into francs. That really threw the
entire bank for a loop. They didn't know the rate of exchange—I swear! I asked three times to make sure I could
believe my ears—so they had to look it up in the paper.
Then Norm watched in astonishment as they scurried
around trying to find five hundred dollars. They looked in
drawers, in cabinets, under stacks of paperwork. Finally,
they scraped up enough francs and proudly turned them
over.) For the entire time we were in France, whenever we
went into our bank, Monsieur Rebattu would stride out of
his office, smile broadly, pump our hands, ask about our
health, and usually give us a calendar or a pen (if anyone
needs six or seven Lyonnaise de Banque wall calendars, just
give a holler). We got a lot of funny looks when we told
people where we were banking, but other than that we
never had a problem. In fact, I've never had better banking
or more personalized service anywhere, proving Red Auer-

bach or Leo Durocher or Vince Lombardi or someone like that to be a genius when he said, "I'd rather be lucky than good."

One of our next points of business was to become fairly familiar with the local wine growers. After a few weeks, we stumbled into a vineyard, only fifteen minutes or so from our house, that sold a local Côte Ventoux. Monsieur Bonnelly et Fils. Monsieur Bonnelly was a man of eighty years or so. As we were tasting his delicious '86 red wine, we struck up a conversation.

"What do you do?" he wanted to know as he was petting Norton. When I told him I was a writer and had, in fact, written about the very cat he was stroking, he asked if I'd ever heard of a Monsieur Beckay. I shook my head and his eyes widened in shock. "Beckay?!" he bellowed. "You've never heard of Samuel Beckay?!!" I finally realized we were having a pronunciation problem. Samuel Beckett is who he was talking about, and when he calmed down I told him yes, indeed, I'd heard of Monsieur Beckett.

"He used to buy his wine here," Bonnelly told me. "Before the war. While he was working on *Waiting for Godot.* He lived in Roussillon and used to come in every Wednesday. He'd buy three bottles of red and flirt with my wife. She was much better looking back then."

Monsieur Bonnelly pulled out a tattered copy of *Attendent Godot.* Not only did Beckett buy his wine there, he wrote about it. In the middle of the French edition of the play, one of the tramps actually says, "Let's go to Bonnelly's for some wine."

Since Beckett is a god to me, in my opinion the greatest writer of the century and the author of the great English novel (a trilogy of novels, actually: *Malloy, Malone Dies,* and *The Unnameable*), this was fairly impressive. Not to mention inspiring. Sparked by the ghost of Godot, we bought several more bottles of wine from Monsieur Bonnelly than we'd originally intended. And as we were leaving, Monsieur Bonnelly called after us. "Perhaps in twenty years, I'll tell people that Monsieur Norton also bought wine from me."

Which is how this book almost came to be called *Meowing for Godot.*

Two of the more interesting local characters whom Norton won over were Gianni Ladu and his wife, Chantal, Sardinian goatherders who ran a rustic *auberge* up in the mountains above Sivergues. Gianni was very much a Sarde, which meant he always had a three-day growth of beard and liked doing nothing so much as slicing open and skinning a goat right in front of you. That could be a little intimidating while trying to have a conversation, I have to admit, but Norton seemed to soften Gianni up a bit. He liked to roam about Gianni's property—not exactly mingling with the goats, but not really avoiding them either. Norton seemed fascinated by those animals' bleats and bla-aaa-aaas, and I got the distinct feeling he wouldn't have minded taking a day-long trek in the mountains with them. Gianni had seen many things in his day, but he'd never seen a cat in his restaurant, especially one who'd hang out with his herd. The restaurant was usually fully booked—they served their meals to a select few at long tables in an ancient room of stone and wood beams—but when I'd call to say we wanted to reserve a table, he'd say, "Is the cat coming?" If I said no, it was fifty-fifty at best that we'd get in. If I agreed to bring Norton, Gianni would usually say something along the lines of, "Okay. We're full—but for you and the cat we have room." We'd then get to sit up in the mountains and eat a whole roasted goat (Norton, for some reason, didn't mind that one of his pals was being consumed right before his very eyes), some of Chantal's homemade lasagna and their fresh goat cheese, and drink way too much of Gianni's homemade *eau de vie*. After a lot of goat and liquor, Gianni's thirteen-year-old son, David, would usually serenade the diners with some ear-splitting Hendrix on his electric guitar, which was a little unnerving for Norton. Other than that, it was a perfect place for a cat to feel as if he were very much the rustic, French mountain *chat*.

~~~

The only unpleasant thing that had to be dealt with quickly after we arrived in Provence was that Janis didn't know how to drive a stick shift. Before coming over, I'd assured her that it was no big deal and that I could teach her easily. She was a good driver, I was a good teacher, what could be easier? It turned out that climbing Mount Everest naked while surrounded by a swarm of killer bees would have been easier. A *lot* easier. There were a few elements of the equation that I hadn't counted on. First of all, it's never a good idea to teach one's mate how to drive. That's a lesson I should have known just from watching sitcoms all my life, but I chose to ignore it. The second warning sign I ignored was that I'm not the most patient person in the world. If I tell someone what to do, I expect them to do it perfectly. I'm aware that that's an unreasonable expectation, but that doesn't stop me from expecting it. The third thing that made our driving lesson difficult was that I'd never quite realized before that Janis was a total nut.

Norton and I took her out in our leased Citroën. Norton hopped into his usual spot, perched on the shelf of the rear windshield. He stretched out, expecting to whizz along to another great lunch spot. Instead, he got taken down to the soccer field below town, the only level place within thirty miles that wasn't a highway.

It had been a long time since I'd tried to teach someone how to shift and use a clutch, but I explained it plainly, simply, and calmly. After the explanation, Janis, who tends to be slightly negative in her approach to life, looked at me and said, "I will *never* be able to do this."

I took these words as a challenge and told her that within fifteen minutes she'd be speeding along the highway, confident as could be.

Two hours later, after lurching around the soccer field, nearly getting squashed by a truck at an intersection, and almost driving off a cliff, I would have told Janis that she was right, she'd never be able to drive a stick, except I couldn't tell her because we weren't speaking to each other.

Norton was not taking sides. Once, when she was trying to pull onto the highway and it looked as if there was a fifty-fifty chance we were going to die, Norton meowed a fairly firm meow. Janis turned and glowered at him, and he quickly decided that meowing was not the way to go. But by the third time I'd made her cry and said something along the lines of, "Even Norton would have learned to get up this hill by now!" Norton would have none of me either. Either I'd offended him by saying *even* he would have figured it out or else he was just fed up with all the lurching about and wanted to go someplace where there was peace and quiet.

The thing was, Janis *had* to learn how to drive. I couldn't be her chauffeur for the year and, despite my assertion, Norton was way too short to reach the car's pedals.

She came through, of course, with flying colors. Once we started speaking to each other again, I reassured her that no one could actually learn all this in fifteen minutes. It would take a few days, perhaps a week, but she would definitely learn. Janis is the type who doesn't like to learn: She likes to be perfect. Since learning, or at least the *process* of learning, is antithetical to short-term perfection, she tended to get rather cranky when doing things like stalling in the middle of a big intersection or coming to a stop at the top of the hill and then rolling half a mile backward before being able to get the car moving forward again. She had the same problem learning French. She didn't want to speak the language until she actually *knew* the language. This was not a very practical approach, not if she ever wanted to go anywhere or do anything. So she gritted her teeth and, not exactly happy but not completely miserable, learned how to drive a stick shift and how to speak French.

Another thing we never anticipated was the French mail system.

It can take two weeks for a letter or package to make its way from America to a small town in the south of France. One of the reasons, we eventually discovered, is because somewhere there is someone who has something to do with French mail delivery who is always on strike. After we'd been there a few weeks, we stopped getting mail. For three or four days straight we'd check the box at the back of the garden and *rien.* Zippo. Not even the *Herald Tribune.* We finally worked up the nerve to ask at the post office and they told us that the Avignon mailmen were on strike. Since Avignon was fifty kilometers away, you might ask yourself what that had to do with us. Well . . . we never quite got a satisfactory answer to that question. The nearest we could tell was (1) most mail had to go through the large Avignon post office before it was sent on to Goult's little, tiny post office and (2) because Avignon was more important than

Goult or any of its surrounding towns, the local Lubéron mailmen were being enlisted to deliver the Avignon mail.

That strike lasted two weeks. When it was over, we got our mail for three days in a row, then it stopped again. On the second day (of the second round) of no more mail, we went back to the post office to see what the story was. The story was that the Avignon mailmen had ended their strike in victory; they'd gotten raises and better benefits. Now the local Lubéron mailmen were striking because they were making less than the Avignon mailmen.

If the mailmen weren't striking, the truckers were striking, which meant no packages could be delivered. If the truckers weren't striking, the railroads were striking, which somehow still meant that no packages could be delivered. If the railroads weren't striking, then the farmers were protesting the horror that's known as EuroDisney and were blocking all the roads and railroads, so no packages could be delivered.

One day, after we'd been in Goult for several months, we noticed once again that the mail had stopped arriving. We trekked back to the post office (all of a two-block trek) to find out who was on strike. No strike, we were told. But our mailman had had an accident. He'd fallen off his scooter— a tiny motorbike, at least a foot too short for his long legs, with the world's loudest engine—and broken his collarbone.

"Oh, that's terrible," I sympathized. "Please send him my best. But what does that have to do with why we're not getting any mail?"

Which is when I realized that there was only one mailman for Goult. If he wasn't able to deliver mail, no one was. He was the only one who knew how to sort the letters, he was the only one who knew where everyone lived, and my guess is he was the only one available for the job who had a motor scooter.

It was two weeks before we got our mail again. And the mailman, a gangly, unhappy-looking man, looked even more solemn than usual as he chugged around town on his motorbike, his arm in an uncomfortable-looking sling.

Norton was, for a while, our only touch with regularity. He was awake and waiting by his food dish at the same time every morning, curled up in the same two or three spots every day, meowing hungrily for dinner at the same time every evening. Everything else in France seemed to us to operate on a whim.

One morning we woke up to find that someone had dumped approximately a ton of rocks in our backyard. This seemed quite mysterious to us, since we were positive we hadn't ordered a ton of rocks. We called our landlady, Elisabeth, in Paris, who was equally mystified. She said she'd get back to us. A week later, the mystery was solved. Several months before, she'd spoken to a *maçon* about rebuilding the stone wall at the back of her garden. She'd asked him to get back to her with a price. He never did. But he did wake up one day, remember that she'd wanted her wall fixed, so he thought he'd just get started. His start was to dump all the stones needed for the job in the yard and leave them there.

After Elisabeth figured out that he must be the culprit, she called him to say that we didn't appreciate the gesture. The next day, he came and gathered them all back up, I assume to dump in somebody else's yard.

Dumping clearly was a major activity in our new neighborhood (or *voisinage,* as I was now learning to call it).

As winter started to settle in, we realized we'd better

store up on our wood for the fireplace. We'd heard all sorts of horror stories of the Provençal wind and cold. When the *mistral* came whistling through the trees, word was that it gave new meaning to the words "when hell freezes over."

We followed a series of crude hand-made signs—WOOD FOR SALE: simple, straightforward, and effective advertising—that led us perhaps a mile away from Goult, to a small farmhouse. The owner shuffled out, smoking a cigarette, beret tipped at the jauntiest of angles over his head, and I couldn't help but notice a disturbing pattern: All small-town French men over the age of sixty-five reminded me of William Demarest.

It's worth bringing up here that there's such a thing as a Provençal accent. It is, in fact, so thick as to render normal French completely incomprehensible, until you get used to its twangs and blangs and various nasal inflections. A Provençal accent puts a "g" at the end of just about everything. The French word for tomorrow is *demain*. With a Provençal accent, it's *demaing*. The word for hand is *main*. With the southern accent, it becomes *maing*. By way of example, take a sentence in English: "When did the man ban guns, John?" An easy sentence, right? Well, pretend you're hearing it for the first time, and with the Provençal accent added to it. It becomes: "Wheng did the mang bang gungs, Jong?" It sounds more like Chinese than English. That's about what Provençalian sounded like to us when we first arrived: some strange tongue spoken only in places where you have to ask directions of Sherpas.

The man selling the wood had the thickest, most impenetrable accent I'd ever encountered. The only thing I was able to clearly understand was when he looked at Norton, who was busy poking around the man's garden, and said, *"Votre chat. Il est très sage."* Several French people made this comment about Norton when we were on our travels. Most Americans, when they meet the little guy, say, "Oh, he's so cute" or "Oh, he's so calm." I much prefer the French way and I think it's indicative of their true respect for cats as well as life: "Oh, he's so wise." *Il est très sage* indeed.

Aside from the flattery about Norton's sagaciousness, after half an hour of conversation this is what I'd learned about the winter wood situation: We either could or couldn't buy it from him. Either his son or his daughter would come visit us or we had to go visit them, although they seemed to live in Spain. If we could get wood at all, it would either come that night, the next week, or never. And it would either cost a million dollars or would be free. When we finally left, my head was spinning, but I was fairly sure I'd ordered a small amount of wood that would be reasonably inexpensive.

I was right about the inexpensive part; I was wrong about the small amount. Three days after our conversation, a dump truck backed up in front of our house, which was no mean feat in itself because the truck fit on our narrow street with perhaps half an inch to spare on each side. When it arrived, the son of the man I'd talked to pulled the lever inside the truck, the back began to rise, and in moments, enough wood to rebuild the Brazilian rain forests came tumbling out onto the street. It took perhaps three minutes for all the wood to empty out of the truck. It then took another two minutes for the truck to make its way back to the end of our street and hightail it out of there. And then it took six hours for me and Janis to carry it, stack it anywhere there was a spare inch—in the three outbuildings in the backyard, in the *cave,* in the kitchen, in the stone hallway by Norton's litter box—and then collapse in an exhausted heap on the floor.

In some odd way, we felt comfortable being in the midst

of such eccentricity. It made us feel a part of the town. And this feeling was magnified because we were accepted by the local Goultoise with surprising ease. We made friends with a French neighbor, who also became our French teacher. She in turn introduced us to another friend, who became our Goult version of Millie in "The Dick Van Dyke Show"—she would pop in at any hour of the day or night; we were free to do the same. She also spent a couple of hours a week teaching us French; we spent the same amount of time teaching her English. And from there, our circle of friends expanded until, by the time we left, we numbered as lifelong friends four French women, one Swedish woman, and two French guys (one of whom became my sports buddy; since I couldn't get my much needed football, basketball, or baseball fix, Norton and I would go to his house to watch the soccer matches. Olympic Marseille became, to me, nearly what the '86 Mets had once been).

We also fell into the extraordinarily interesting expatriate community that populated the Lubéron. Most were Brits, a few were American. Expatriates are usually running away from something. Some from work. Some from politics. Some from relationships. Almost all, in one way or another, are running away from themselves and feel that a new life in a new place, particularly a place like Provence, will help them re-create themselves. Sometimes they like to start from scratch, sometimes just partial replacements are needed.

Almost every expatriate we met had some sort of secret. There were messy divorces in their pasts. Some had left husbands for younger men. Some had left *wives* for younger men. There were vaguely sinister stories: violent ends to affairs; suicide attempts; the mysterious loss of millions of dollars. Everyone we became friends with had a vague shadow hanging over them—and that made them all the

more interesting. It made them appealing. Couple that with
the fact that they'd all made the same choice we'd made—to
leave one life behind and resettle in a French paradise—and
it created an instant bond, one not felt to this extent, from
my end, since I'd been given a certain six-week-old Scottish
Fold kitten.

We went with these people to the opera house in Avignon to see Mozart concerts and we practiced our French
reading from the *Provençal,* the local newspaper equivalent
of the *National Enquirer* (their favorite thing to write about
is how many people were killed and injured on the highway
during the week: 4 MORTS ET 7 BLESSÉS! is a typical head-
line of the *Provençal*). We went to harpsichord concerts in
local churches and trudged to Avignon to see English-language movies. We hiked for miles with them, exploring the
wonders of the mountains, and went on treasure hunts and
once, on a magical New Year's Day picnic, even danced
around in a circle, holding hands, singing the words to "Sur
le Pont d'Avignon" (although if you tell that to any of my
close, personal friends, I'll deny it). We stayed up late nurs-
ing them through broken hearts, we lived through their
affairs with married men, we ate in their homes and cooked
for them. We told jokes—in various languages—and made
one another laugh. And we slowly learned a lot about a
group of people—English, American, French, Swedish, you
name it—with whom, ostensibly, we had nothing in common, yet grew to treasure.

Not all of our treasured memories, however, revolve
around people. Or even cats, for that matter. Every so often
there were other—if you'll excuse the expression—catalysts
working their magic.

By far the strangest and, in some ways, the most delightful experience we had the entire time we were in Goult was
when Janis came running into the house late one afternoon.
Excited, she told me to hurry up, get Norton, and jump in
the car. She wouldn't tell me what was going on, she just
insisted I follow instructions.

She drove—she was becoming quite proficient with the
Citroën and by this time could almost get up a steep hill
without my head banging against the windshield thirty or
forty times—until we came to the town of Menerbes, another perfect Lubéron mountain village, ten minutes away
from Goult.

Just outside the town, Janis stopped the car to let an
animal cross the street in front of us. It was a goat. I was
about to say, "What's a goat doing in Menerbes?" when I
looked to the right of the car and saw two lions lounging
by the side of the road. Next to them was a friendly but
quite large elephant. Before I could get too disoriented,
Janis drove a little further and we came to a small tent that
had been set up. In front of the tent was a man in a clown
outfit and five or six small children running around in front
of him, giggling and yelling with pleasure.

"We're going to a circus?" I asked Janis in disbelief.

"We're going to a circus," she answered.

I would love to report that this charming country circus
was an artistic triumph, everything that the overdone and
overhyped Ringling Bros. type of show is not. Unfortunately, if I did report such a thing, I'd be lying through my
teeth. This little circus that Janis brought me and Norton to
was the cheesiest, most pathetic, most hilarious thing I'd
ever seen in my entire life.

The human troupe consisted of a ringmaster, two clowns,
and a woman acrobat who, every time she so much as did

a simple somersault, looked as if it was going to be her last act of life. She tripped and fell down *twice* while walking across the arena to encourage us to applaud the ringmaster. The clowns also were not of the highest possible caliber. One clown's wig kept falling off, and you could tell he wasn't happy about dressing up in the stupid-looking costume anyway. The other clown's sole job was keeping the bouncy music going, but the tape machine was on the old side, so the music wasn't all that bouncy because it was played somewhere around two speeds too slow. When it came time to bring the speakers inside—they'd been outside to help broadcast the exciting news that the circus was in town—the whole troupe chipped in. It was a struggle for all of them to lift the things—enough of a struggle that they almost knocked the entire tent over in the process.

Once the show started, things managed to get lots worse. The opening act was Minou the Dog Genius. Minou's trainer (the ringmaster) strode out into the middle of the ring, announced that we were about to see the smartest dog in the world, then, with a deep bow and a majestic wave of an arm, called for Minou to come running. No such luck. Minou was either asleep or hadn't been paid in a week, because there was nothing they could do to get that dog into the ring. The ringmaster kept calling him, but Minou never showed up. Finally, one of the clowns had to carry the pup into the tent and plop him down in the center. The ringmaster then told the genius dog to leap up onto a stool—and he announced to the audience that we were going to see the most amazing mental feat ever performed by a member of the canine race. It really wasn't as amazing as all that—because all Minou did was turn around and run out of the tent again.

The ringmaster began to realize that Minou was off his

performance that night, so he called for JoJo the Brilliant Horse. Norton enjoyed JoJo tremendously, especially when JoJo refused to do anything except trot around the ring. "Up, JoJo!" the ringmaster would thunder, and JoJo would trot some more. "JoJo! How much is two plus two?" the ringmaster asked. Unless I lost count and JoJo trotted around the entire ring four times, I don't think he had any idea how much two plus two were. That didn't stop the ringmaster from thanking everyone for watching JoJo the Brilliant Horse (*"Mes amis, messieurs, mesdames, les enfants, JoJo le cheval génie!"*), and then introducing The World's Most Intelligent Monkeys. Their entire act was to eat their dinner as fast and as messily as they could in front of the rapt crowd.

By the time of the monkey act, Norton was getting a little bored. I'm sure it was beginning to occur to him that if these animals were making a decent living, he could become a millionaire without too much trouble if he ran away to join a French circus.

That was when he got his moment in the sun.

There were not a lot of people in the audience. I'd say perhaps twenty small children, two or three mothers, and us. But when I heard the ringmaster say, into the mike, *"Monsieur! Monsieur, s'il vous plaît,"* I really didn't think anything of it. Not, that is, until Janis pointed out that he was talking to *me,* since I was the only adult *monsieur* in the joint.

"Monsieur," he repeated, when he finally caught my eye. "Come here," he said. *"Venez."*

If I knew what I was in for, I don't think I would have brought Norton into the ring, but I truly wasn't expecting anything other than semi-funny banter. Even if I did have to participate in something physical, I figured I could just eat some food quickly or jog around the ring twice when they asked me how much one plus one was. Even when they brought the camel center stage, I still didn't understand what I was supposed to do. Only when the camel knelt down and one of the clowns led me over to it, did I realize I was supposed to get up on the thing and ride it around the tent.

Norton was a real trouper, I'll say that for him. He let me hold him as the clown boosted us up onto the camel's back. I held on to the cat with one hand and on to the camel's hump with the other. As the *dromadaire* sped faster and faster around the ring, and Norton got more and more relaxed, the children in the audience went wilder and wilder. Out of the corner of my eye, I'm pretty sure I saw Janis laughing uncontrollably, though she swore to me later she was impressed with how well I'd maintained my dignity.

The main thing I remember is the ringmaster, who realized that with all his trained elephants and monkeys and horses and dogs, a nonprofessional cat was stealing his show. To his credit, he went with it. Standing off to the side, he began bellowing into his microphone as we rode past and the cheers grew louder and louder and Norton sat up straighter and straighter on the back of the camel. "Ladies and gentlemen, boys and girls," he was saying. *"Messieurs et mesdames, les enfants, mes amis! Je vous present le monsieur et son chat extraordinaire!"*

a cat on the riviera

One of the strangest things about living abroad is being away from home for holidays.

I'm fairly big on tradition. Every Christmas Eve I go to my friends Glen and Sharon's apartment for dinner. Every December, on the first weekend of the month, I throw a waffle and champagne party and make everyone I know watch *It's a Wonderful Life*. Thanksgiving is my favorite holiday of all and for ten years I've been going to other friends, Kathleen and Dominick (of the traumatic Search for Norton Day), to eat a major feast, drink many bottles of delicious port, and play a killer game of charades. In general, I'd have to say that Thanksgiving is my very favorite day of the year.

In France, Thanksgiving doesn't exist. I experienced this once before, when I went to college at the University of London. I gathered a few American students over at my flat, along with some newly acquired British friends. It turned out that none of us Americans had a very firm grasp on exactly what Thanksgiving was. We knew it had something to do with the Three P's: Pilgrims, Plymouth Rock, and Pocahontas. And we were pretty sure we were supposed to be giving thanks for religious and political freedom and for the fact that only in America could there be an official holiday that enabled some creative entrepreneur to actually make millions of dollars off those little orange and black candy corns. Other than that, all we knew was we were supposed to eat a lot of turkey and pumpkin pie. (Although pumpkin pie is not a well-known treat in England and, being college kids, we didn't really know how to make one—so we tried doing it with a real pumpkin rather than canned pumpkin. It's difficult to describe the actual taste of our dessert that night. The closest I could come, I think, would be to say it had the delicate texture of a terry-cloth robe and the subtle taste of a whole lot of unsweetened chocolate.) To this day, I think there are several English people walking around London who think that every final Thursday in November, Americans celebrate a bizarre Pilgrim-Indian sex rite by eating terrible food.

We did slightly better in France, though not at first.

Two weeks before the big day, we went to one of the two butchers in Goult—we'd settled on one we preferred, though for no logical reason—and told him we'd like to order a turkey *(un dinde)* for the end of November.

"You mean the end of December," he said.

"No," I said. "I mean the end of November."

"That's impossible," he told us.

"And why is that?" we wanted to know.

"Because the turkeys are not fat yet," he said.

It turns out that no one in the south of France ever eats turkey except for Christmas. So, especially in such rural areas as the Lubéron, November and December are months spent feeding the birds and getting them plump enough for *le diner de Noël.*

"But it's a very important American holiday," I explained to Monsieur Isnard, our butcher of choice. "What if we order a pathetic thin turkey?"

Non.

We debated having a Thanksgiving feast of chicken and shallot tart, but we were spared such an agonizing break from tradition when our friends Nicholas and Linda called and told us to come up to Paris to have Thanksgiving with them.

Nicholas is French and Linda is American and they've been living in Paris for five years now. They also have twin five-year-old daughters, Naomi and Gala, possibly the most gorgeous, sweetest children who ever lived. At the time, they were refusing to speak so much as one word of English, even though Mom was American and they absolutely could understand anything spoken in English that they wanted to understand. Instead, they would look adorable and speak perfect French, saying such cute little *enfant*-like things as, when riding in the car on a cold winter day, *"Oh, maman, j'adore la musique et la chauffage!"* which means, "Oh, Mom, I adore music and the heating system." I know it doesn't sound nearly as good in English, but nothing does, and when they'd spew out these accented epigrams, my heart would melt so quickly it was pathetic. So we were in the mood to see Linda, Nicholas, and the kids anyway, and our choice was made easier yet when we took into consideration that Linda was a cook of the first degree. So it was on to Paris for Thanksgiving.

The TGV—*train de grande vitesse* ("train of great speed," or "big, really, really fast train," as I like to call it)—has changed everyone's life down in Provence. In the old days, it was a seven- or eight-hour train ride from Paris to Avignon. By the time you got to the train station, waited for the train, stopped a hundred times along the way, and got to your final destination, it was an all-day trip. Now, with the fast train, it takes three hours to get from Provence to Paris, and you get there in extremely luxurious fashion. The drawback is that wealthier and more annoying Parisians are now able to consider Provence something of a weekend retreat. On the other hand, it makes it awfully nice to live down there, knowing how simple and hassle-free it is to get up to the greatest city in the world.

Norton was a big TGV fan. Human seats need to be reserved but pet seats don't. And because the train is built for comfort as well as speed, there are thick, plush armrests which, when pushed down, make the perfect seating arrangement for Scottish Folds. Norton could stretch out on the armrests and do his favorite thing in the whole world: stare out the window at the countryside as the train sped along at a hundred miles an hour. Since it was only a three-hour trip, he didn't even need a litter box.

This was our first weekend in the big city since we'd moved down to Goult, and we decided to live it up. We stayed in L'Hôtel, a very beautiful hotel on the left bank on the rue des Beaux-Arts, celebrated because it's the house where Oscar Wilde died. It's even possible to stay in the very room—and bed—Oscar Wilde died in, although why anyone would want to do that I'm not exactly sure. The rooms are tiny (unless you take the suite on the top floor, which is huge and looks like a very classy nineteenth-century whorehouse; unfortunately, the cost is more like a twenty-first-century whorehouse) but are filled with antiques and decorated in lots of bright red and green velvet.

The colors somehow work, though they tend to be just a tad overpowering. In fact, as the bellman was opening the door to our room, he said softly, *"J'espère que vous aimez la couleur rouge"*—"I hope you like the color red." It was a fair question because *everything* in our small room was bright, shocking red. The wallpaper, the bedspread, the chairs, the towels. We got used to it in a few moments, but I must admit that for several days after we left, everything we saw looked rather drab and bland.

As usual, the hotel was totally taken with the cat. Within minutes of checking in, the concierge sent up a bowl of milk for Norton's cocktail hour. Just to be on the safe side, I checked to see whether Janis or I had gotten any fruit or chocolates, but as usual it was only *le chat* who received any complimentary calories.

The first day we were there, we did a lot of Christmas shopping at the antique stores along the nearby rue Jacob and, farther away, rue St. Paul in the Marais. One St. Paul store particularly impressed me. They remembered me from previous shopping sprees—usually to bring something back to Janis when I felt particularly guilty about being there without her—and even remembered most of the things I'd bought there over the years, which I have to admit made me feel about as sophisticated as I can feel. They clearly had no idea what my name was but they did remember my shopping companion. When I strolled in with a cloth bag on my shoulder and a gray cat poking his head out of the bag, they greeted us with the warm words, *"Bonjour, monsieur! Et bonjour, Monsieur Norton! Ça va?"* It never fails.

The night before Thanksgiving, Norton met his French *attaché de presse*. *The Cat Who Went to Paris* was being published in France before too long and the editor, an Ameri-

can woman named Nina Salter who was an editor at the
Parisian publishing company Albin Michel, decided it
would be wise if Norton met the woman who'd be doing
the publicity for the book.

Janis, Norton, and I went to a restaurant called Le Square
Trousseau, a smoky bistro populated with a lot of publishing and show-biz types, near to the Bastille. Nina and
Kathy, the publicist, were regulars but the place was jam-
packed, so even at nine-thirty at night we had to have a
drink at the bar before being seated. No problem for Norton. He took a stool at the end of the bar, his little head
popping up over the brass railing. Kathy sat next to him,
petted him, and clearly fell in love. What's not to love, I
guess. Norton's a great date.

Dinner went smoothly as the relationship between Norton and his publicist proved to be the real thing. Norton sat
in his own chair, and nothing going on around him dis-
turbed him—not the noisy crowd, not the giant St. Bernard
who camped under his chair almost the entire evening, not
the patrons of the restaurant who, periodically, would come
over and ask me if that was a real cat.

Kathy made his life a lot easier—and mine a lot harder—
by giving Norton the full star treatment. She hand-fed him
some of her foie gras, then some of her chicken. For dessert,
she ordered him a plate of chocolate ice cream (it was far
superior to that of Bistro d'Albert). As an after-dinner
drink, she ordered him some milk and, since he is the
world's sloppiest milk slurper, Kathy even wiped his mouth
with her napkin after each session with the milk bowl. That
was the final straw as far as Janis was concerned. For months
afterward, she complained vociferously that no one ever
wiped her mouth after she ate. I tried pointing out that
perhaps someone would if she would agree to bend down

and eat out of a bowl, but she never took my advice to heart, which was probably all for the best.

The next day, we were all slightly hung over. Janis and I from too much wine and *eau de vie,* Norton from too much spoon-fed foie gras. We were content to linger in our red velvet room for most of the morning. I was especially content because there was a TV in the room and I'd been having sports withdrawal down in Goult. Much to Janis's horror, I watched a Pistons-Pacers basketball game on an English cable station, then, much more to her horror, proved how desperate I really was by watching almost all of a Hulk Hogan versus The Undertaker wrestling match. Our only interruption came when two of the hotel maids knocked at the door. Janis told them we'd be out of the room in another hour or so, but they weren't there to clean—they were there to introduce themselves to Norton and play with him. We told them we'd leave him in the room for the afternoon so they could pet him to their heart's content.

That night was Thanksgiving dinner over at Linda and Nicholas's apartment. I believe this was Norton's first official Thanksgiving (he's never gone to Kathleen and Dominick's because they have two cats, Lulu and Zonker, who don't cotton to any feline competition in the annual charades game). He was made to feel welcome by the twins, Naomi and Gala, who crayoned little place settings for everyone. They drew a picture of me and set it in front of my plate on the table. They did the same for Janis and for their mom and dad. For Norton, they drew a lovely picture of him, complete with flattened ears, and put it on the floor, right next to my chair, along with a bowl which happened to be perfect for holding bite-sized morsels of turkey scraps.

The dinner was a grand success. In Paris it was not only

possible to get fattened turkeys at the end of November, it was possible to get everything needed for stuffing and sweet potatoes and mashed potatoes and all other Thanksgiving delicacies.

By the end of the weekend, we felt we'd had a touch of home, which we'd needed. Norton felt as if he'd had a *new* home since, when we checked out of L'Hôtel, I believe that every single employee came to say good-bye to him and wish him *bon chance.*

~~~

Norton, Janis, and I had the next several weeks to ourselves, during which we continued our Provençal explorations and our Provençal ritual of stuffing our faces at every possible moment. And then, right at Christmastime, a new ritual began: Company started arriving.

Our first guests were—and don't start any gossip, this was strictly a platonic arrangement—my friend Norm Stiles, the "Sesame Street" maven, and my friend and book agent, Esther Newberg, the well-known cranky person. Neither Esther nor Norm had ever been to Provence before and we were determined to show them how perfect life could be.

It wasn't as difficult as we thought.

It turns out it's not hard to convince people that life is perfect—not when they're in Goult for Christmas.

The lights in town are, of course, tasteful and elegant. Strings of colored lights ring the tower of the church in the lower part of the town; a strand of white lights sits over the thousand-year-old vaulted arch that leads to the town *château.* Along the main street, artfully decorated lights run, every ten yards or so, across the width of the street, from one building to another.

In our cozy house, we got two Christmas trees—a large

one for the living room and a small one for my third-floor (or second-floor, if you're French) office. Both trees were decorated Provençal-style: with various fruits (tiny tangerines, which are called *clementines,* small apples, and pears) and strands of nuts.

On Christmas Day, Janis, Norton, and I strode around Goult, enjoying the simple fact that we were there and nowhere else. Norton started out in his shoulder bag but before long hopped out and walked with us. The town was fairly empty—even the tiny caged birds were inside—so we had a relaxed cat on our hands, one who was ready to stroll anywhere.

We passed one house we'd admired since the day we'd arrived. It was off a small grassy triangle at the top of the main street, before one reached the castle. From the outside, Janis had picked this as her favorite place in town—it was quite old and at one time had been the Goult post office, but had obviously long ago been converted to a spectacular home. They'd been doing some work on the house, fixing up the courtyard, and I'd peeked my head through from time to time, admiring and envious. On Christmas Day, as we passed by, a grungy-looking workman in overalls was busy poking and scratching at the stone outside the house. The doorway leading to the courtyard was open, so I pulled Janis in to show her the work that had been done. The workman looked at us but didn't say anything, but after it was clear that we were so admiring of the place, he asked us if we wanted to see the rest of the house. Since looking in other people's houses is our favorite thing in the world, we immediately said yes. The workman started leading us through the entire home, which was much larger than it looked from the outside and even more spectacular. It was restored magnificently and furnished to the period, the late 1500s. After twenty minutes or so, we arrived at the kitchen. Sitting around the kitchen table were two women—clearly a mother and daughter—and two young children. The younger of the grown women looked at us—two strangers, a workman, and a cat—and asked the workman what he thought he was doing. The workman replied that we—the strangers and the cat—had admired the house and he thought we might like to see it. She sighed, they discussed the situation, and pretty soon Janis and I realized that the workman wasn't a workman—he was the owner of the house. We'd just managed to worm our way into his family's Christmas celebration.

We immediately apologized and tried to leave, but now the family would have none of it. They insisted we see the rest of the house, which got better and better with each room we toured, then they made us stay for a drink (okay, okay, they didn't *make* us, but it would have seemed inhospitable just to tour and run). The man who'd been showing us his place turned out to be a Belgian architect who lived, most of the time, in Algiers. This magnificent home was his weekend retreat, which he used only three or four weekends a year, plus Christmas week.

After our drink, we realized Norton had wandered off to examine the house on his own. I'm sorry to report that I panicked briefly; in that house he could have hid for days at a time and I had a sudden vision of not only ruining these people's Christmas but their New Year's as well. Luckily, he came the moment I called him, hopped into his shoulder bag, and Janis and I took him back to our house on rue St. Frusquin.

It was still relatively early, and we decided now it was time to open Christmas presents. Janis and I exchanged first. I got an ancient hanging oil lamp (I have a fetish for old lighting fixtures) as well as something I'd been looking to get for myself for over five years: a beautiful bowl and matching pitcher to go in a wooden dry sink I'd bought long ago. I'd never been able to find one I liked, but Janis had spotted this at the weekly antique mart in L'Isle-sur-la-Sorgue and hidden it away some weeks before. She received, in turn, an eighteenth-century iron (she has the same fetish for old irons that I have for lamps) and two nineteenth-century casserole dishes in the shape of hearts. Aaaaahhhhhhhh.

Norton did all right, too. He received several cans of Pounce (which I'd had someone send to me from New York; good cat treats are the one thing France seems to lack) and two fine catnip toys, one in the shape of a mouse, one in the shape of French bread.

For dinner that night, we did it up. We invited several Goultois to join us and devoured our very own fat turkey, chestnut stuffing, *patate douce avec cognac* (sweet potatoes drowned in brandy, to you), and some of the old toothless crone's killer goat cheese.

All in all, it was a perfect French Christmas and we were now ready to face Americans.

The next morning, we drove down to the Marseille airport, an hour away, to pick up Esther and Norm. They are both very dear friends and we were thrilled that they were our first guests, but, to be fair, I've got to paint a realistic picture. Neither of them had ever been in the European countryside before. This was Norm's very first trip to France. Within moments, he was so overjoyed at being there, he was speaking "like zees: I luf ze French. Zay are ze best. Oui!" and thinking that he was already able to communicate with the French on their own level. Esther, on the other hand, is not a person who's very comfortable when she's away from her office (picture a small, tightly wound Ethel Merman and you'll have the picture—I won't have an agent, but you'll have the picture). By the time we got back to Goult, she had three faxes waiting and two urgent calls to return. So while we showed them their rooms and helped them get settled, Esther spent an hour on the phone negotiating various deals and Norm walked all over the garden, speaking to the trees and stray cats in some language he was convinced was French. "Allo, leetle tree, 'ow aire yew? Et bonjour, Monsieur Bird. Eet ees very nice tew see yew. *Oui?*"

Our rule of thumb with jet-lagged arrivals was that they had to stay up until ten P.M. That way they'd be exhausted, would sleep through the night, and would wake up refreshed and back on a regular schedule at nine or ten the next morning.

That afternoon we took them to a cocktail party at our neighbor's (she was English; it was a Boxing Day party). Then we took them up into the mountains to Auberge de la Loube. We were the only people in the restaurant that night, so they moved a big table right in front of the fireplace. Norm toasted everybody and everything, while Esther dozed off in her chair (in addition to jet lag, she was also carsick from going up the winding road to the restaurant). Norton was now on such friendly terms with the three dogs that he hopped into their hiding place under the hearth with them for much of dinner.

We had a few days to be tourists with our guests and we enjoyed every moment of it. The next day, we began running them around to all our favorite places. We made them climb to the top of Oppede-le-vieux, a medieval village dominated by wonderful ruins at its peak. There is a straight drop from the cliff when you get to the top of the town. I, myself, never ventured too close, but Janis liked to teeter on the edge and drive me crazy. Once, while she was doing that, a private airplane flew by *below* her. The passengers waved while I held on to a tree, getting dizzy just thinking about it.

After Oppede, we had lunch at an amazing *routier* called Bistrot du Paradou in the very small town of Paradou. The restaurant is a four- or five-hundred-year-old stone house divided into two dining rooms. The front room has an enormous bar, usually surrounded by local truck drivers swigging wine and *pastis* and telling stories. The back room is perhaps twenty tables along with a fireplace, which usually has a *rôti* going, with lamb or chicken or rabbit on it. In wintertime, the Bistrot is only open for lunch, and only during the week, and each day they serve only one thing. You call up and ask what their menu is that day and they'll tell you they're having a *pot-au-feu* or an *aïoli* (which they have every Friday) or a *coq au vin* and then you decide if that's what you feel like eating that day. They also serve a delicious salad and as much red wine as you wish to drink (the bottle's waiting for you on your table when you sit down; it's produced directly for the restaurant and is *biologique*—organic—which means there are no sulfites or other nasty chemicals). The owner was a successful advertising executive who decided one day he'd had enough of selling Perrier or whatever it was he was selling, so he opened up the perfect fantasy of a French restaurant.

The Bistrot du Paradou is one of Norton's top three Provençal restaurants as well as ours. I think this is due to a combination of the fact that one particular waitress there likes him very much and is always telling him how much

smarter he is than her dog, and the fact that the hearth is
so large, Norton can sit almost anywhere in the whole
restaurant and be warmed by the blazing fire.

After lunch, we went several miles down the road to the
best olive oil mill in all of France, the cooperative mill in
the town of Maussane. Maussane happens to be Janis's favorite town in the south of France, with the possible exception of St. Remy. It's built right onto the road, is small and
charming yet extremely sophisticated, and looks exactly like
the kind of place where Sergeant Saunders always used to
get wounded in the show "Combat." More to the point,
their olive oil is so delicious that we have personally risked
lengthy prison terms smuggling many liters of the stuff back
to New York.

After watching them crush olives, then buying enough
oil to pan-fry half of Western Europe, we drove back to
Goult. That afternoon, we had a party of our own, a cocktail
party from five until whenever, so all our new friends could
meet our two old friends. We had about thirty people in all,
some Brits, one expatriate American, a couple of Swedes,
and mostly French. We served leftover turkey and a giant
ham and lots and lots of delicious cold *champagnoise* from
the *cave* in Coustellet, but the biggest hit was the bagels and
cream cheese that Norm and Esther brought from New
York. The French people thought this was the most delicious thing since the invention of the croissant and gobbled
down the onion bagels like there was no tomorrow.

The biggest surprise of the party was not that all our
friends got along so well. It was that Norton, for the very
first time in his life, not only spent most of the evening
attending a party, he let all the children there come up and
pet him.

I have not discussed the dark side of Norton's personality, mostly because there really isn't one. If he has a flaw at all, it's that he doesn't much like children. Small children, to be exact. I suppose it's understandable. Children are very volatile and loud and move in sudden herky-jerky motions. As a grown-up, I find them scary enough, so I really can see why Norton has always shied away from them. If we're in public, which we often are, Norton doesn't hiss or scratch them or anything like that. He simply gets very passive and withdraws into a shell, or else, if he's able, he'll make sure to just stay out of their way. At our first major Goult cocktail party, however, we had many children underfoot. They ranged from five years old to twelve, and somewhere around eight at night, I saw Norton calmly sprawled on the living-room floor, letting one of the five-year-olds try to crayon the top of his head.

France was clearly having its effect on the star of my family. And I must say I approved.

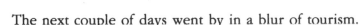

The next couple of days went by in a blur of tourism.

We all went to Arles and tried to find some semblance of Van Gogh but, except for the ultramodern Van Gogh Café and a Van Gogh gas station, hardly a trace remains. It is a beautiful town, however, and Norton was fascinated by the bullfighting school that practices in the town's Roman coliseum. We also went to Avignon, a truly great city. I don't know if Norton was able to appreciate the Palais du Papes or the spectacular wall that rings the town or even the Utopia, the only English-language movie theater south of Paris. I do know he definitely appreciated the *manège*, the merry-go-round, that sits in front of the opera house, gloriously lit, and spins around all night. Norton would have been happy to sit there with it, watching it go until dawn.

We took our visitors to the market at L'Isle-sur-la-Sorgue, of course, where we bumped into every single person we knew in Provence. By the end of the shopping trip, I'm sure Esther and Norm thought we'd bribed total strangers to pretend that they knew us and fake our guests into thinking we were popular. After buying our weekly supplies, we then took a wine tasting trip to Châteauneuf-du-Pape, which was only forty minutes from Goult. (In case no one seems to be making the connection between all these places with the word *pape* in them, here's a very brief and probably inaccurate history lesson: When the French government was trying to, more or less, take over the Vatican, they wound up installing their own Pope and luring the Catholic Church headquarters over to France. When you tour Avignon and Châteauneuf, it's not really hard to see why they came running. The palaces are awe-inspiring and the wine is, arguably, the best in the world. When the corrupt French Pope finally died, he was replaced by a corrupt Italian Pope who went back to Italy, but the palaces and the wines remain, with Avignon as their approximate center. End of lesson.) Janis and I had made several trips out Châteauneuf way and even knew some of the owners of the smaller vineyards (we're easy to remember: There aren't many American couples who come wine-tasting with a Scottish Fold). Typical of the Provençal French—of their class, their warmth, and their style—one of the *cave* owners we'd previously spent time talking to about wine gave a half bottle of his newest vintage to Esther and one to Norm as presents. He also offered one to Norton, but I decided my cat had already picked up enough bad habits and, since Norton was technically a minor, I declined for him.

By the time Monday rolled around, Esther and Norm

were fairly convinced that we were living in paradise. And then we decided to *really* go wild.

One of the best things about Goult was its location. Not only was it in the heart of the magnificent Lubéron, it was a two-and-a-half-hour drive from skiing in the Alps, it was two and a half hours down to Barcelona, it was two hours from Nice and Cannes, and it was two and a half hours to Italy. So we decided to have an adventure and go visiting foreign lands.

Norton had already spent lots of time in Italy and down on the Riviera. Nice (which is pronounced Neese; trust me: This will come into play later) was one of his favorite towns in France. He liked the accommodations, the food, and found the Niçoise particularly friendly. We'd been down there often, partly for business, mostly because we had friends living there.

An old friend of mine was Joel Douglas (Kirk's son, Michael's brother, a successful film producer in his own right). I'd known Joel and Michael when we were youths and had kept in touch over the years. Michael, of course, went on to become a zillionaire movie star and Oscar winner and even see Sharon Stone naked (for which I would happily give up the zillions and the Oscar). Joel wound up living the perfect life, moving to Monaco, marrying a terrifically nice woman from Nice (or neese woman from Nice; uh-oh, don't get me started), and was running the oldest working film studio in Europe, which he and Michael were in the process of buying. (Just to clarify: They were buying the studio, not Europe, although I have a feeling Michael could afford to actually buy the Continent if he so desired.) I was talking to them about doing some work out of the studio, so after we'd been in Goult a few weeks, we went down to talk some new business as well as catch up on old times.

Norton, Janis, and I met Joel and his wife, Paddy, at the commissary at the old Victorine Studios. After a very tasty lunch and even tastier conversation—we hadn't seen each other for years and had a lot to catch up on: brothers, parents, work, ex-girlfriends or ex-wives as the case may have been—Joel took the three of us on a tour of the studio. I was in heaven, because Victorine is like an old Hollywood studio from the twenties and thirties. It's got all the atmosphere and magic and romance that studios used to have (they still have them in L.A. to a certain extent, but it's all tempered by the fact that Sam Goldwyn and Harry Cohn have been replaced by either agents, morons, or corporate Japanese people). On the lot we saw the places where they filmed Truffaut's *Day for Night* and Hitchcock's *To Catch a Thief,* and the greatest French movie of them all, *Children of Paradise.* Joel also showed us a rough cut of a promotional film they were putting together about the history of the studio. It was put together by the studio projectionist (whose father was the studio projectionist, as was his grandfather. This guy *lives* for the studio). Unfortunately, despite the best of intentions, it was a *very* rough cut—dominated by a lot of unknown actors in period wigs—but the screening room was very luxurious. After half an hour or so of the film, Norton stretched out on the chair next to mine and took a little cat nap.

That night, we had dinner at a fish restaurant with Joel and Paddy and their small, very friendly if somewhat over-active dog. Norton and the hyper pup got along quite well, though Norton spent a little more time on my lap than he usually does.

The next day, we strolled around Old Nice, where I

could happily live. The new part of Nice couldn't be uglier (actually, that's not true, it could be Cannes, which is perhaps the ugliest beach city in the world), but Vieux Nice is full of cobblestone streets and ancient churches and wonderful little shops and restaurants. Since it's so close to the border, only fifteen or twenty minutes away, Nice is as much an Italian city as it is a French one, and the combination definitely works.

Norton made several trips to Nice while we were in France and, while that may be his city of choice on the Riviera, I think he found St.-Jean-Cap-Ferrat a close second.

The day we went to Cap-Ferrat—or as I like to think of it, "The Village That Only Donald Trump Can Afford to Live In"—we were visiting Nina Salter, the editor of the French edition of *The Cat Who Went to Paris* (the translated title: *Le Chat Qui Dinait Chez Maxim's*). It's not that French publishers pay their editors so much more money than American publishers do, it's that Nina was visiting a childhood friend of hers, whose parents had a nice little mansion in Cap-Ferrat, right on the sea.

Norton took to it immediately, ignoring the scrumptious repast that was set before us when we arrived, preferring to stroll the grounds and sniff out the new surroundings. After lunch, he came for a walk with us, along the boardwalk and up into the rocky crags of the shoreline. Norton was not as foolhardy as Nina, who dove into the sea and took a lengthy swim (this was in early March, when the temperature was all of forty degrees). My little cat much preferred the dry rocks and, while various swimmers trembled and turned blue, Norton found the only ray of sun to luxuriate in.

It really *is* hard to argue when someone says that cats are a lot smarter than people.

Norton also spent some time in the ultra-chic town of Ramatuelle, just outside of St. Tropez. An author and friend of mine, Edward Behr, was based in Paris but had bought a house in Ramatuelle in 1966, for something like forty dollars. It was a modest little joint: a one-time hotel with six or seven bedrooms, a professional kitchen (including walk-in freezer), an uncountable number of dens and offices, a balcony overlooking St. Tropez and the Mediterranean, and, surrounding the swimming pool, sloping gardens that rivaled those at Versailles. That's all.

Norton, jet-setter that he is, liked Ramatuelle fine, but he really took to St. Tropez, where he got to sit on the bay and sip—or, more accurately, slurp—a *café liegois,* a fancy name for a cross between an iced coffee and a coffee sundae, the first nonchocolate concoction I've ever seen my cat flip over.

All of this is by way of pointing out that Norton was a far more experienced traveler in the south of France than either of our Christmas Week human guests.

The first thing we decided to do with Esther and Norm was to stop off in Nice to walk them through the old town. This we did, and all went smoothly, except for the moment when Norm, forgetting once again that he couldn't speak French, got into a conversation with a shopkeeper. He was buying a few presents for people back home, and the woman at the store asked him a question in her native tongue. Norm, still refusing to acknowledge that he didn't understand the language, nodded and responded, *"Oui. Un peu."* (Yes. A little.) This confused the woman no end, since the question she'd asked was, "Would you like this gift-wrapped?"

You try gift-wrapping something just "a little."

Being the ultrasophisticates that we were, we decided to

venture into Italy for lunch. We also decided that spontaneity was the way to go for this brief two-day trip—we would just do whatever the hell we felt like for thirty-six hours. Naturally, the first thing we felt like doing was eating. So we drove half an hour to the town of Ventimiglia, the Italian/French equivalent of Tijuana.

Janis, Norton, and I had done this trip several times. Nothing made us appreciate our year more than saying, spur of the moment, "Let's drive to Italy for lunch." And Ventimiglia happens to be a perfectly nice town. It's not Rome or Verona or Venice, but it *is* Italy, so what could be bad?

We had a delicious lunch right on the sea. Norton got his own plate of scampi and the restaurant made him feel so at home, he did a little wandering, checking out a few of the other diners, moseying into the kitchen to see what else he could dig up in the way of antipasto. After lunch, we did what people seem to do in Italy: We spent two hours waiting in line at a bank trying to change our francs into lira, and then we went to an open-air market to buy yet more food. The only hitch in this part of the operation was that Norton single-handedly almost started World War III.

As we walked into the market, the little guy was in his usual position, sitting up with his head swiveling out of his shoulder bag. The Italians feel just as warmly toward cats and dogs as the French do—they see nothing even remotely strange about a cat visiting a restaurant or a market—so as soon as we stepped inside, one of the vendors sprang into action and offered Norton a fresh sardine. Norton looked at him as if he was insane, sniffed at the fish rather rudely, and turned his attention elsewhere—mostly toward the *gelato* stand.

"What's the matter with him?" he asked me. "He's too good for my fish?"

"No, no, no," I hurriedly assured him. "He just doesn't *like* fish."

"He's a cat, isn't he?" the fish vendor wanted to know.

"Sure, he's a cat," I agreed.

"Then he should eat fish."

"I know he should"—and here I shrugged very philosophically; that usually worked with French people—"but he seems to be more of a meat eater."

I should point out here that what I was speaking was NormLanguage. I don't speak a word of Italian, so I was mixing in a little French with a little English, and a lot of a Vito Scotti–like Italian accent.

"This is a *fish* market," the guy now pointed out to me. By this time, several other vendors had gathered around to see what the commotion was. No one was happy to see it was a cat who didn't eat fish.

"Yeah," another one grumbled. "Why bring a cat who hates fish into a fish market?"

Smiling at all of them, I mumbled to my cat under my breath, "Norton, sweet little cat, *please* eat the sardine."

No chance. My sweet little cat simply doesn't eat fish. But the vendor held it out in front of him again and Norton practically gagged. Before there was a full-scale riot, Janis wandered over, took me and Norton by the arm (and paw), and led us back out into sunlight and safety.

"*What* was that all about?" she demanded.

"He's got fussy eating habits," I said, pointing to our gray companion. "It's not his fault."

"No, it's not *his* fault," she said and rolled her eyes, leaving no doubt whose fault she thought it was.

Full and now feisty—and still living on spontaneity—we

all piled back in the car and decided to keep forging further into Italy.

"What about the French Riviera?" Esther wanted to know.

"Italy's great," I told her. "It'll be fun. We'll just drive until we get to someplace nice and then we'll find a hotel."

"What about a reservation?" she asked, and we all explained to her, once again, this whole concept of spontaneity. Reluctantly, Esther agreed to go along with the crowd.

And the crowd proceeded to drive into five hours of hell.

We checked a map and decided we'd go on to San Remo, a supposedly nice resort town, supposedly only another hour or so further into Italy. Note the key repetition of the word *supposedly.*

The first part of the drive went smoothly. Then, as we approached San Remo, we noticed that traffic was slowing down. The last mile or so into town took a little longer to travel than it should have—by about an hour. The next thing we knew, we were on the outskirts of San Remo stuck in the worst traffic jam in history. The first half hour, we were all calm. The second half hour, Janis went to sleep. We had now progressed about a hundred feet into town. The third half hour, Esther started to whine. The fourth half hour, Janis woke up again and she joined in the whining. We were now all of a hundred and ten feet into town. Somewhere in there, Norm snapped. He began talking in a thick Italian accent, pretending he was a native of San Remo. "Excusa me," he said, tapping on the window as if he were outside the car. "I'ma liva here an' Ia been inna my car fora fourteen years. The radio no work—hassa anything happened?" I started giggling, which was a bad sign, and only egged him on. The Italian accent continued. "Excusa me. I justa bringa my new son homa from the hospital. It taka me eighteen years and now I have to finda the college." By the time Norm was through with his riff, we learned that no one in the town of San Remo had ever been out of their cars, no one in town knew how to walk, and that forty-two percent of the town's population had the first name of Fiat. This went on for nearly an hour (or another hundred and fifty feet). Janis and Esther were in a total panic by this point. They not only hated being in traffic, they hated me and Norm, who were laughing so hard as to be near some strange form of mental illness. Norton was the only one keeping his head, but I maintain it's because he was in the backseat with Esther and Janis and simply didn't want to face their wrath if he started laughing along with us.

In addition to his take on San Remo, Norman also explained a word game he'd invented several years before when the Ayatollah Khomeini was first popping up in the news. Norm was obsessed with the whole Ayatollah/Salman Rushdie business ever since he found out that Salman Rushdie had gotten engaged. Norm figured that he, Norm, went out almost every night in search of the perfect woman—or even a date who'd see him a second time—and had never been able to find her. Now, here was a guy who was in hiding, under the threat of death, and he was getting married! My pal Norm didn't think this was fair or just. So he created a game about the Ayatollah hoping perhaps an entire religion would put a price on his head and he'd get to meet an attractive woman.

The game he invented was that you had to come up with a new type of Ayatollah, defined by his job or his attitude, but one who rhymed with Khomeini. For instance: The Ayatollah who loves dogs is the Ayatollah Great Daney.

The Ayatollah mystery writer is the Ayatollah Ed McBainy. The weird Ayatollah is the Ayatollah Insaney. Okay, granted that on paper it might not look like much, but after hours of being stuck in the car with crazy Italian drivers honking their horns every fifteen seconds, it was the greatest thing that had happened to me since I was twenty-one years old in St. Tropez and saw a gorgeous blond woman walking along the beach wearing nothing but sunglasses, a thong bikini bottom, and white cowboy boots. For the rest of our trip—which at the time seemed as though it would probably be spent on the not-all-that-attractive road leading to San Remo—I became obsessed with rhyming Ayatollahs. Some of the better ones: The accordion-playing Ayatollah (the Ayatollah Lady of Spainy), the mogul Ayatollah (the Ayatollah Citizen Kaney), and the spitfire-singing Ayatollah (the Ayatollah Abbe Laney). My guess is, if I keep this up much longer, my editor will cut all the rest of them out anyway, so I think I'll stop here with the Ayatollahs.

We did finally get out of San Remo, at which point Esther seized control of the situation. We stopped at a not-fancy-looking hotel, desperate for accommodations. It wasn't seedy but it also wasn't the Ritz. Esther strode in and asked if they knew of a nice hotel anywhere in the vicinity that had a room. They asked if she wanted a room there and she said no: She wanted a *nice* hotel. (Okay: Here's where that whole Nice pronunciation comes in handy. The same way I overdid the Thanksgiving jokes when Janis and I were once in Turkey, I became a little too vigorous about switching the uses of Nice, the city, and nice, the adjective. I can't tell you how many times one of us would say, "That looks like a nice restaurant," and I would respond, "Do you mean a nice restaurant or a Nice restaurant?" I can't really defend myself on this matter, but I found it funny every single time this came up in conversation, until Janis told me that if I said "Nice" for "nice" one more time, she'd kill me.) Anyway, despite Esther's insult in the roadside hotel, she did find out that we were never going to be able to stay anywhere on the coast of Italy that week. It turns out that the whole country has Christmas Week off for vacation and, apparently, everybody *in* the whole country comes down to the coast. What was causing the traffic jam is that there is exactly *one* coast road. That's right. If you want to get anywhere on the Italian (or French, for that matter) Riviera and you don't use the highway, there is one tiny, winding road and that's it.

It didn't take us long to change our plans. We turned around immediately and headed back to Nice (which seemed like it would be nice). There we decided to treat ourselves to a magnificent evening, since our day had been so completely miserable. Instead of staying at the nice (sorry! I can't help myself) but small and moderately priced hotel Janis, Norton, and I usually stayed at, we checked into the Negresco. And we didn't just check into the Negresco—we checked into the most expensive, luxurious, over-the-top two-bedroom suite they had. For you prudes in the reading audience, don't worry; Esther checked into a third room far down the hall. She didn't want to be anywhere near any of us.

We went to a lovely restaurant, Coco Beach, right on the water, and had a perfect fish dinner. The owner—I know you'll think I'm making this up, but he really did remind me of a French William Demarest—prepared a few grilled shrimp for Norton when he got word that the cat wasn't wild about regular fish. The shrimp seemed to do the trick. As a matter of fact, ever since Coco Beach, Norton has been willing to chow down on all shellfish as well as the occasional bite of salmon. Tuna, however, remains out of the question, as do sardines.

After dinner, we went to the Nice casino. (Don't worry: My lips are sealed. I will make no comment on whether the casino was . . . ummm . . . pleasant or not.) Norm was the big winner. Not only did he pocket several hundred dollars, he came up with the world's stupidest Ayatollah (the Ayatollah No Brainy).

The next morning, we drove back to France along the glorious Mediterranean, stopping off in Eze, probably the most touristy village of its type but nonetheless a spectacular medieval town that cannot be missed. We had lunch at the Grill du Château at the very top of the town, where the waiter went crazy over Norton.

"*Votre chat,*" he told me. "*Il est superb!*" He was the first cat, the waiter gushed, he'd ever seen behave like a human being.

That night was New Year's Eve and we spent it back in the Lubéron in fine style. We had a few French friends come over for some champagne—no *champagnoise* that night!— then the five of us went to Auberge de la Loube for their special New Year's dinner.

I've already described the delectable appetizers at the Auberge, but on New Year's Eve Maurice puts on a special spread. It starts with a truffle omelet—two or three eggs scrambled with the scrapings of wild, black French truffles, mushrooms so strong and delicious they are considered one of the great delicacies in the world (and priced accordingly, although Maurice doesn't charge for this dish—it's his gift to his regular clients). I don't think Maurice was all that thrilled when I gave Norton a taste, but he softened when he saw how much Norton enjoyed it.

The rest of the dinner was on a par with the *truffes,* then

exactly at midnight, Maurice poured champagne for everyone and we all toasted and hugged and meowed appropri-
ately, welcoming in the New Year.

Thursday was Esther's and Norm's last night in Provence, so naturally we had to eat even more food by way of
a fond farewell.

I'd lost a bet to Esther before leaving for France—I'd said
that Clarence Thomas wouldn't be confirmed; she told me
I was a naive ignoramus and, of course, she turned out to
be right—so my payment was to take her to Oustau de
Baumanière, the legendary restaurant which is the best and
most famous in this area of Provence.

Janis and I had been there before. The owner and chef,
Jean André Charial, is a friend of Wolfgang Puck's and so
I'd heard about this place for years and years. In fact, it's
thanks to Baumanière that Janis and I really wound up in
Goult. Several years before, we had stayed at the hotel (it's
not just a restaurant; it's one of the great hotels in the world,
too). As if the feather beds and down comforters aren't
enough of an enticement, the town of Les Baux is spectacu-
larly set into white Bauxite mountains. When you first see
the town, and the hotel right outside of town, it's as if
you're Ronald Colman in *Lost Horizon* and have just found
Shangri-la. Over the years, we'd stayed and/or eaten there
several times. Since we'd been in Goult, we'd made the
forty-five-minute drive a couple of times to worship at the
feet of the two-star chef. More important, Baumanière was,
no question about it, Norton's favorite restaurant. The staff
loved him and usually greeted him with affection and a bit
of wonderment. He was automatically given his own chair
when we were seated at a table, and often had a special
dinner prepared for him.

This night, the restaurant outdid themselves, both for humans and for cat. Esther agreed she'd never eaten a meal like that, even in her dreams. Norm could barely say he'd had a Nice time. Janis, as usual, kept her dignity until the huge cheese cart arrived, then she lost any sense of propriety and basically just kept screaming out, "More! More! More!" to the server. Norton was served a small dish with three separate specialties—duck, scallops, and fish. At Baumanière, even Norton will eat the fish.

The *pièce de résistance,* as usual, was the dessert.

Each of the humans had ordered a specialty of the house—a hot soufflé, covered in *crème fraîche* and the appropriate sauce (if a raspberry soufflé, raspberry sauce; if chocolate soufflé, chocolate sauce; if gingerbread soufflé, their newest and possibly greatest creation, gingerbread sauce). Each of the soufflés is presented on a covered silver dish. The soufflé is brought before the diner, placed on the table, and then with a flamboyant but spritely motion, the cover is whisked away and the customer usually goes something like "Oh my God!" or "Ooooooooohhhhhhhh!" or, if you're our friend Dominick, "Is that all?!"

Four times we witnessed this ritual, first for Janis, then Esther, then Norm, then me. Then we realized there was a fifth silver dish and it was placed directly in front of Norton.

Before I really had time to ponder what they could have possibly made for my cat—a Pounce soufflé??? a Whiskas Chopped Chicken and Cheese soufflé????—the waiter whisked off the silver cover to reveal a small, gray, marzipan mouse, complete with tail, pink eyes, gray whiskers, and black marzipan nose.

The creation drew well-deserved applause—not just

from us, from other appreciative diners as well—and the pastry chef received Norton's permanent and undying gratitude.

Deep down, despite all the proof to the contrary, I know that Esther, my own agent, thinks I make all this stuff up about Norton. This night, I made a special point of watching her as she stared at the cat, who was calmly taking a few licks of his mouse on a silver tray in a two-star French restaurant as if this were something he was used to every night of the week. The look in Esther's eyes at that moment told me it was almost worth having Clarence Thomas on the Supreme Court. Not quite but almost.

The next day, my gourmet cat was most sorry to see Norm and Esther go back to New York. It meant that life, for him, was going to return to normal.

Or as normal as Norton's life ever gets.

a cat in spain

For the month of February, my old pal and writing partner, David, came to pay us a visit. It was not entirely social; we were writing a screenplay together and we decided there was no better place to write together than in my temporary office on the third (or second) floor overlooking the Lubéron valley.

In a sense, history was repeating itself as far as David and I were concerned.

So many years ago it's a little depressing, we went to the south of France together for our first collaboration. He had just graduated from journalism school and was taking a year off to travel in Europe with his girlfriend. I had just finished writing my first novel and was certain it was only a matter of time before I would be rich, famous, and a celebrated literary man about town. I was young and headstrong and thought I could do anything. One of the things I thought I could do was to quit my first real job at a publishing

company and my $135 a week salary and go off and spend
a year in the south of France. This was a concept carefully
planned and maturely thought out in the manner of most
of my plans in those years: David and I got extraordinarily
drunk and stoned on a train ride from Boston to New York
and at some point during the five-hour trip, we decided
we'd rendezvous in Europe and write a movie together.
This was in 1976.

Several terrific things came out of that train trip. We
actually did write a movie together, which was flat-out hor-
rible, but which eventually was sold as a television pilot,
helping us to break into that charming business. We're still
writing partners, after all these years, which was another
nice result of that fifth or sixth Jack Daniel's on wheels. The
best thing that happened, of course, was that we wound up
rendezvousing just north of the Spanish border halfway in
between the towns of Collioure and Port Vendres, which
was about as close to heaven as two young, broke, would-
be-screenwriters and novelists could possibly come. We had
a dirt-cheap apartment and we could actually jump from our
balcony into the clear, blue Mediterranean (we never did,
but we *could* have, if we were really the Ernest Hemingway
clones we thought we were instead of two fairly cautious
Jews who didn't want to have to learn the French phrase for
"Excuse me, do you have a very large bottle of iodine and
several hundred yards of bandages?"). We shopped at the
open-air market, which magically appeared in the Port Vendres square every Saturday, and bought fresh fish direct
from the fishermen during the week (Port Vendres was still
a mainstream fishing village in those days). Wine was
twenty-five cents a bottle and we were too young to have
ever heard about cholesterol, so we basically spread cheese

on anything or anyone we possibly could. Nobody in town spoke a word of English, the temperature seemed to be eighty degrees every single day, and there was one great café in Collioure, an amazing place called the Templiers, which astonishingly had original Picassos on the wall because old Pablo and Braque and Matisse used to trade paintings for food when they were mere pups (or *petits chiens,* if you want to be technical) and lived down there. We went into the Templiers every single day after we were done writing, for a cognac or a *pastis* or just a cold beer, and when the eighty-year-old owner of the Templiers actually deigned to shake our hand one day when we came in—the ultimate sign that we were considered regulars and were now accepted by the town—we knew that, indeed, life was a very, very good thing.

We were young and even though we ran out of money in several months and had to return to New York—my novel had indeed sold to a publisher, but I learned the harsh truth that while an advance paid for a first novel does allow one to actually buy meat once in a while, it doesn't allow one to lead a Scott Fitzgerald–like lifestyle—I was under the impression that this was the way my life would be lived from then on. I did not appreciate that the daily handshakes at the Templiers and the Brigadoon-like fog of perfection surrounding Collioure were not things simply handed over on a regular basis to anyone who thinks he deserves it. It was the zenith, the goal that one strives for throughout one's life. It was, in a sense, a dream, but it was a dream I had actually experienced—and one I would not and could not forget.

Clearly, since I was now, sixteen years later, doing my best to repeat it.

I'd even gotten my old buddy Dave to repeat it with me. And what better way to do this than by returning to our old stomping grounds? With Janis and Norton, no less.

~~~

Janis had heard our romantic rhapsodizing and seen several million photos of Collioure over the years. She also knew me and David too well, and was aware that as soon as we were back in the town for a weekend, we'd be laughing our heads off over things unexplainable and want to see places that had no interest for anyone who wasn't personally involved in the sightseeing. So she decided that Collioure could not be our one and only destination. After a brief discussion, we all agreed to stop off in Collioure Friday night, spend some time there Saturday, then drive on down into Spain for the rest of the weekend. We settled on Barcelona as our final destination, as neither Janis, David, nor Norton had ever been there.

France has changed quite a bit since David and I first discovered what it was like to live there. French people now use English words like *parking* (as in "Make ze first right and zen go to ze parkeeng") and *fax* has actually been given a gender (it's male, in case you're interested—*le* fax). Plenty of McDonald's do, indeed, dot the landscape, and French politicians are now more or less as corrupt as their American equivalents. (They probably were always corrupt but it seemed as if the corruption always revolved around sex and food. Now French corruption has been Washingtonized and the scandals have become financial.) Even so, we were not prepared for our first look at the 1990s version of Collioure.

It looked a lot like Miami Beach.

When we'd lived there, it had been a sleepy village. It

was a resort town but was not considered chic or hip and was known mostly to French people who lived in the southwest part of the country. We lived in one of the few modern apartment buildings; it was on the southern outskirts of town and was one of perhaps five or six buildings in the complex. Now, as we pulled up in our Citroën, it was almost impossible to see the village, which was completely hidden behind a skyline of giant condominiums. It was a lot like the scene in *It's a Wonderful Life* where Clarence the Angel takes Jimmy Stewart back to Bedford Falls to see what it would have been like if he'd never lived—and sleepy, all-American Bedford Falls has turned into Pottersville, where every other store is a nasty-looking saloon and naked dancing girls are everywhere you turn. Perhaps Collioure wasn't *that* bad, but it *was* a shock to the system. Everything was new and everything was ugly. Janis had that look in her eye, the one that said, *"This is the place you've been telling me about all this time?!"*

I didn't panic, however, and my patience was rewarded once we made it into the old part of town. The French may put up truly ugly new structures, but at least they don't tear down the old beautiful ones in the process. The old village was left untouched and was exactly as David and I remembered it. Once we were safely ensconced within the medieval walls of Collioure, everything was fine.

We had booked rooms at the hotel Templiers. This was not a coincidence—the Templiers was the place with the Picassos and Braques and Matisses, our old watering hole. When we lived in Collioure, we had never been able to afford to eat there, much less stay there, though the old man, Monsieur Pous, had once shown us through the whole building, pointing out some of the famous artists whose paintings also adorned the hotel walls and corridors.

The restaurant was Norton's kind of place. Very casual, very friendly, a little bit of sawdust on the floor. An excellent eatery for a cat to wander through and poke around in.

David and I were thrilled to be eating there. It was as if we'd been in there drinking our *kirs* just the day before. Some of the old-timers sitting playing cards at the back table even looked familiar. Exactly as we remembered, every inch of the walls were covered with paintings and sketches. Some of them were awful, some of them were wonderful. Some were done by absolute nobodies—if *I* gave the owner a drawing or painting, he'd put it up; and, believe me, my artistic ability stops at stick figures—but some were, incredibly, original Picassos. Right in the middle of the room was a large photo of Monsieur Pous, the owner, with his arm around Pablo himself. Framed with the photo was a Picasso line drawing of a reclining nude.

One thing had changed, sadly, in the years since we'd last been there: The old man, Monsieur Pous, had died. But his sons now ran the place, and they obviously had a keen sense of tradition. We were glad we'd had the opportunity to shake Monsieur Pous's hand back when we were young, and we'd seen enough of the way he'd run his place to know he'd approve of the way his family was carrying on.

The meal was exquisite. Norton came back from his tour just in time to share my plate of grilled squid and garlic, and stuck around long enough to have a reasonable amount of my bouillabaise. He didn't taste any of the local wine, which was very dry and very good. (In fact, the wine from Collioure is now the latest "hot" wine in France. It's still fairly inexpensive and really is delicious. It makes me proud to realize that many years ago I used to practically bathe in the stuff.)

The next day, David and I took Janis and Norton on a

nostalgic trip through our past. I sensed that Janis was a little bored but Norton seemed interested. His head was out of the shoulder bag the entire trek. I think he was glad to find that I'd actually lived a life before he'd arrived on the scene.

We took them first around the old village. We went into the *pâtisserie* I used to go into every morning to buy breakfast. Every single day for three months, I'd go in and ask for *"deux pains au chocolat"*—two chocolate croissants. Unfortunately, my *"deux"*—two—sounded like *"du"*—some. So five days a week, four weeks a month, for three full months, I'd ask for *two pains au chocolat,* and each one of those days the woman behind the counter would smile and say, "Very well, monsieur. And how many would you like?" It didn't matter how I pronounced the *"deux,"* it didn't matter that I sometimes repeated it three times, as in, *"Je voudrais deux, deux, deux pains au chocolat"* and hold two fingers up in front of me. Every single time she would ask me how many I wanted and every single time I'd want to kill myself because I couldn't make her understand my French. Years later, a dear friend of ours in Goult, Danie, showed me how to distinctly differ my pronunciation when saying *"du"* and *"deux."* Still psychologically scarred after all that time, I worked up my nerve, went into the Goult *pâtisserie,* and asked for *"deux pains au chocolat."* "Very well, monsieur," the woman behind the Goult counter said. "And how many would you like?" Crushed and humiliated, I went running to Danie for consolation. She told me how to avoid this problem forever after: I should, from here on in, order *trois* pains au chocolat!

We walked out to the old stone lighthouse and in and out of the town's alleyways and cobblestone paths. In these sections, nothing had changed at all and that stability was, to me, remarkably reassuring and exhilarating.

After we got through walking Janis and Norton all over town, we drove out to see our old apartment building. This was the worst change of all. It was no longer one small ugly building surrounded by four or five other small ugly buildings. It had turned into a giant and horrendous apartment complex. There were probably a hundred and fifty hideous condos built at the spot. We still were excited to see it—although Janis couldn't understand why we'd get excited visiting the ugliest place she'd ever seen in France.

By late Saturday morning, we'd gotten the past out of our system and were now ready to head to Spain.

Collioure is only a few miles north of the border. We drove past Port Vendres, which was just as lovely as we remembered, past the towns of Banyul and Corbere, and then we were in Spain. Or nearly in Spain.

Going from France to Italy with a cat is no problem. In fact, the Italian border guards never even look at Norton when we drive there. The same for Switzerland. Luckily, I'd brought Norton's papers along, because it turns out the Spanish are very strict about bringing pets into their country.

"You have a cat," one of the six border guards told me.

"*Si,*" I said. (Spanish is one of the many languages I also don't speak. I tried French and English and even a word or two of Italian, hoping one of those would work. They didn't.)

"He has a cat," the guard now said to another guard. Why they needed six border guards when clearly ours was the only car that had passed through all day was beyond me. But I didn't want to ask. I was already in enough of a jam.

"*Si, si,*" one of the guards now chimed in. "*Uno gato!*"

"Do you have the papers for the cat?" I was now asked.

It turned out I *didn't* have the papers for the cat. I had

papers, but not the right papers. In Spain, you need some special permission from the embassy or some such place. But, happily, the guards didn't really have any idea what the right papers were either.

"He has papers," one of them announced.

"Are they the right papers?" another one asked.

"I don't know. They're in English."

"Ask him if they're the right papers."

"Señor," the first guard now asked me. "Are these the right papers for the cat?"

"Yes," I lied and nodded very convincingly.

The guards relaxed and smiled—all six of them—and waved us through.

Now we were in Spain.

Our first stop was Cadeques, one-time home of Salvador Dali as well as a lovely northern beach town. The drive there was fairly uneventful, except that the road was particularly winding and curving and both Janis and David got kind of woozy. They wound up in the backseat feeling sorry for themselves. Norton sat happily beside me, the perfect passenger.

After lunch in Cadeques, we took the *péage*—the high-speed toll highway—to Barcelona.

Barcelona may be the perfect European city. It's small, stunningly beautiful, very sophisticated. The people are friendly and the food is delicious. And they like cats. As I said: perfect.

Norton toured the city with us from morning till night. He saw the spot from which Columbus set sail for America, he took a walking tour of the Barri Gòtic (the Gothic Quarter), he visited several Gaudi buildings, including the still-being-constructed Sagrada Famillia cathedral, he ate a special Catalanes paella for dinner at the restaurant La Cuineta.

Then, to top it off, he—and we—saw one of the great sights of the western world.

In front of the cathedral, which dominates the square in the center of the majestic Gothic Quarter, we witnessed a hundred Barcelonians dancing the official dance of Barcelona—the almost indescribable "sardana."

Night had just arrived, candles were flickering on the tables in the outdoor cafés, there was mystery and romance in the darkness and shadows. Suddenly ten circles formed, rings of ten people each. Every member of the circle held hands, the hands raised triumphantly above their heads, and all had replaced their regular shoes with white espadrilles. The ritual had begun. They stood like this, motionless, for perhaps thirty seconds, then an orchestra, tucked into a corner of the massive square, began playing lively, sensual, exquisite Spanish music—and then a hundred grown-ups began spinning and dancing and flailing exactly like Jerry Lewis on the bandstand in *You're Never Too Young.* It was the scariest, most inane sight I've *ever* seen. If a hundred people did this in New York, I guarantee they'd be beaten to a pulp and then arrested—and deservedly so. Forget the ritualized beauty and power everyone talks about. Forget all that passionate blood coursing through Spanish veins. I'm telling you, this was worse than the clog dancers on the Labor Day telethon.

That more or less ended Norton's first visit to Spain. I believe a statue was later erected after our weekend trip, commemorating the very spot on the square where an American tourist actually laughed so hard, he almost passed out.

We did stop for lunch on the way back, at a tiny café on the coast. The sun was shining, so we sat outside and drank sangria while Norton ate to his heart's content off an enormous plate of grilled shrimp.

The waiter came by at some point; he stood over our table without saying anything, watching the cat. Finally, he turned to me and said, "Your *gato*. He is Spanish?"

"No," I told him. "American. By way of Scotland."

The waiter stayed by our table for another few minutes, watching Norton munch on the *gambas*. Before he turned to go back to the kitchen, the waiter tapped me on the shoulder, then pointed at Norton.

"He is handsome enough to be Spanish," he announced.

We finished our sangria, gathered the cat up, and headed back for the car and for France.

"You are handsome enough," I said to my little gray pal. "Just don't try puttin' on those espadrilles. Even *I* have my limits."

Forty-five minutes later we were back on French soil, where the border guards didn't ask to see Norton's papers, only welcomed him into the country with a very polite *"Bonjour, Monsieur le chat. Ça va?"*

It felt a lot like coming home.

a cat in Italy

8

At some point, before we settled on Provence, there was a very good chance that Norton was going to have to learn Italian.

I think he would have adjusted with few qualms. For one thing, he's very happy with Italian cat food. He still won't eat Petreet's *Tonno con Riso* (although I definitely would, in a pinch; it looks *good*), but the Gioie di Miao version of *Pranzo Regale con Gamberetti* is, judging from the way Norton attacks it, as good as anything he's had in the finest restaurants. He even enjoys, when the mood strikes, the Italian dry food, the Brekkies *con pollo* and *con manzo.* And Norton usually feels about dry food the way I feel about movies where Barbra Streisand plays the sex object.

Norton's spent a lot of time in Italy over the years, as have Janis and I. Since Goult was so close to the border, and since all three of us had travel in our blood, we spent a lot of time in Pastaland during our year abroad.

Our first foray came only a few weeks after we'd arrived in France. We went down to Nice to visit our friends the Douglases, and the next morning, instead of turning back and heading home, we ventured twenty minutes further away and went to Italy for lunch.

The moment you cross the border, everything changes. The French plant in straight, orderly rows. Their vineyards are organized and perfectly manicured. In Italy, nothing is straight or orderly. Everything looks as if it's been planted by Foster Brooks. Five minutes away from France, the cheese is completely different, the vegetables are different, the whole way of life is as if it's another planet.

This was always difficult to explain to our Goult friends, who usually thought we were nuts when we'd tell them we went to Italy for lunch or drove to Barcelona for the weekend. That's not something they ever would have done. We would explain that in America you can drive for three days straight, and still be in the same country and the same basic culture. If you start in Goult and drive for three days straight, you're in a completely new world.

So we would pop over to the border town Ventimiglia for lunch on occasion, usually to the *ristorantes* La Caravella (on the water) or Cuneo (right in town; very near the market where Norton refused to scarf down a sardine). At Cuneo, the proprietors, Beraudo and Figli, were particularly nice to Norton. By the end of our first visit, it was clear he was free to wander through the restaurant; what was theirs was his. One thing I'll never know is how or why cats pick their favorite spots, but pick them they do, and at Cuneo Norton's favorite spot was underneath a large, elaborately carved wooden hutch. That's where he'd eat and that's where he'd stay until we'd polished off every last drop of our Chianti.

The first time we made this sojourn to Italy, we had a little surprise waiting for us back in Goult.

We left Ventimiglia soon after lunch, at three-thirty or so, and arrived in Goult at six P.M. As we pulled into town, we were a little startled to find somewhere around two hundred and fifty people—approximately a quarter of the town—marching around the streets, up, over, and down, starting and ending at the Salle des Fêtes (literally, the Holiday Room, but what it is is the town meeting place, where they have everything from political rap sessions to the weekly bingo festivities). As if it weren't strange enough to find the whole town on parade, they were being led by twenty guys dressed like Richard Burton at the end of *Beckett*. They had on red and green robes, pointy hats, and were wearing religious-looking insignia and necklaces. As if *that* weren't enough, they would stop walking every ten feet or so and blow into long trumpets, blaring something vaguely heraldic. Every time they stopped and blew, the whole town would cheer wildly.

Needless to say, we parked our car and joined the rally, curious to see what could possibly be going on. I assumed Goult had won the French version of the World Series or else it was Bridget Bardot's birthday, which I'm sure must be a national holiday over there. It turns out I was wrong on both counts. The guys in the red and green robes were The Brotherhood of Wine Growers (those religious necklaces weren't religious or necklaces, it turned out: They were silver wine-tasting cups), and this was the annual march to celebrate the new vintage Côtes du Ventoux wine. They didn't just march, either. They gathered the whole town in the Salle des Fêtes and handed out free glasses of red, rosé, and white to anyone who wanted to taste it. We followed the parade from beginning to end, went into the

Salle des Fêtes, happily drank our glasses of wine, shook hands with the silly-looking guys in the robes (there were also two silly-looking women in robes, to show how far the French have progressed), then we went home, wondering if this is what would happen every time we went off to Italy for a day.

It wasn't. But that didn't stop us from going there. And we did venture further than Ventimiglia on several occasions.

My mother came over from Los Angeles to visit us for a while. We decided, on the semi-spur of the moment, to take a few days off and head toward Tuscany, which, unbelievably to us, was only a five-hour drive away. Going there is like driving from New York to Boston, except when you arrive you don't have to listen to Red Sox fans feel sorry for themselves. Plus the food's a lot better.

Our first stop was the town of Levanto, in the provence of Liguria, and the hotel Stella Maris (Roger's wife—and yes, I did say that at the time, and yes, Janis did swat me on the arm). The hotel is really nothing more than a bed and breakfast, slightly run-down but very cozy, and only a block from the beach, which is nice in season. But what really makes it special is that there are huge and spectacular sixteenth-century frescoes all over the ceilings, and the people who run the hotel make you feel as if you're a member of their family. Norton was the first cat who'd ever stayed there and at first they didn't know what to do for him. They kept knocking on our door and offering food, then milk, then they knocked just to see if he was content and comfortable.

We'd had a bit of trouble finding the Stella Maris the night we pulled into town. After driving aimlessly for a few minutes, we decided to stop at a café and see if we could

figure out how to ask directions. The café we stopped at had
nothing but Italian men standing around swigging down
beer and anisette. Norton and I went in to see what was
what. At first, the guys in the café stared at me as if I were
from Mars. Not because I had a cat on my shoulder, but
because I kept asking for a street called the via Marconi.
After a while, one of the grizzled regulars came over to me
and said, "Via *Ma*rconi?" "Sì, sì," I said. "Via *Ma*rconi."
They all got a major laugh about the fact that I thought such
a street might have been pronounced via Marc*o*ni, and then
the real laughs started when they tried to give me directions. At some point, the same grizzler took me by the arm,
put his hand on Norton's head, and yanked me out of the
bar and into my car. He then shoved Janis over, climbed in,
and began barking out orders that we interpreted, sometimes correctly, sometimes not, as things like "Go!" and
"Right!" and "Left!" After fifteen minutes, he said something we were pretty sure meant "Stop!" and when I did,
he hopped out of the car, disappeared around a corner,
and we found our car parked right in front of the hotel
Stella Maris.

Our second night in Italy, we stayed in the truly extraordinary town of Lucca and in the even more extraordinary
hotel (a misnomer; it really is a castle), Villa S. Michele.

Villa S. Michele was originally built in the fourteenth
century, added on to in the seventeenth century, and has
been magnificently restored by the owner, whose name
actually was Giuseppe, an Italian charmer in his late fifties
or early sixties.

We spent the day touring Lucca, an old walled city that
has to be seen to be believed. After many months in the
small and relatively unsophisticated environs of Goult, we
were surprised at how sophisticated and stylish the Italian

version of the Lubéron really was. The chicest thing one
could buy at the L'isle-sur-la-Sorgue market was a fancy
apron. In Lucca, built into the ancient stone and rock, were
row after row of designer clothing stores. Even Norton
seemed to get a little bit of a lift spending the day around
so many gorgeous and well-turned-out people.

At lunchtime, at another superb Italian restaurant,
Bucadisantantonio, Norton was paid the supreme compliment. The four of us were quietly making oohing and ahh-
ing noises over our pastas (or our small ashtray full of
diced-up grilled chicken, depending on whom we're talking
about), when I noticed a man at a nearby table doing nothing but staring at Norton, who, as usual, was sitting next to
me on his own chair, eating and minding his own business.
I smiled at the man but he didn't smile back—he just kept
staring. Finally, after he and his wife paid their check and
stood up to leave, he hesitated, then approached our table.
He said something to me in Italian and when I indicated
that I didn't understand, he asked whether I spoke French.
When I nodded, he said, as solemnly as could be, *"Votre
chat, monsieur. Il est très sage."*

Your cat, sir. He is very wise.

Yes, I agreed. I'd been told that before. Very wise. And
the man, content to have paid homage, turned and left the
restaurant.

We got back to the hotel, exhausted, having covered
every inch of Lucca on foot (Norton was sound asleep in his
shoulder bag long before we made it back to the hotel).
When we arrived, the owner/restorer was behind the desk.
He was a friendly sort, so when we asked for our key, he
started talking, asking us what we'd done all day, etc., etc.
As we were starting to trudge upstairs to our rooms, for

some reason he stopped us and said the magical words, "Do you like to eat?"

I don't know what made him ask that. Perhaps it was the strands of pasta that were still dangling from my mouth, several hours after lunch. Perhaps we just had that lean and hungry look (well, hungry look, anyway). Either way, his eyes lit up when I said to him that yes, not only did we like to eat but that my mother was a fairly well-known cook and cookbook writer back in the United States.

Our new best friend got incredibly excited.

"Where are you going for dinner tonight?" he asked, and when I told him, he shook his head and said, "No, no, no." Then he paused and asked, "Do you like truffles?"

We all looked at one another, shrugged, and went, "Sure." (By the way, this conversation was not as easy as it looked—our new pal didn't speak a word of English; we compromised on a fairly rocky bastardization of French.) "I will take care of you," he announced and immediately went to the phone, dialed, waited a few seconds, then spoke rapid Italian for several seconds and hung up. He turned to us proudly and said, "I called the best restaurant in the region, told them a famous chef was coming, and told them to prepare a masterpiece for you!" He then insisted that we come down an hour before dinner, so he could serve us a drink and some cheese.

After a brief nap, we rendezvoused back in the lobby and met our new protector. He took us downstairs to his private bar, in the hotel's *cave,* where he poured an ice-cold local white wine for an aperitif. Just in case we weren't going to eat enough food at the restaurant he was sending us to, he also cut some slabs of fresh Parmesan cheese and homemade sausage (which Norton thought was the single most delicious thing he'd ever eaten).

Our host, Giuseppe, had thinning white-yellow hair, thick black-framed glasses, and wore a black turtleneck. He looked like a worker; his hands were rough and strong when he slapped you on the back (as he was wont to do) or clasped your hands in friendship. He was extremely energetic, full of life and lust (I'm fairly sure I caught him batting his eyes at dear old Mom once or twice). He also loved to talk, and thus told us his entire life story. He spoke French because he'd learned it in school. While studying, his teacher had given him the name of a girl in Paris—a countess. They exchanged letters (supposedly as language practice) and he fell in love, going back and forth between Rome and Paris to see her for eighteen years. (I don't know what happened after the eighteen years. At that point in the story, I started to be able to think of nothing else but how delicious that cheese was and concentrated on eating as much as possible before we had to leave for the restaurant.) He used to run a modern hotel on the island of Elba, then decided to come to Tuscany, where he renovated S. Michele over a period of three and a half years (it had just opened a few months before we'd accidentally stumbled in there).

By the time we'd polished off his bottle of wine—for which he refused to charge us—it was time to leave for our truffle extravaganza. It turned out to be far more than we had bargained for.

The restaurant Solferino, just outside of Lucca, was nothing fancy. Quite the contrary. It was a family-run joint, divided up into seven or eight small rooms. The bar was filled, as so many Italian places are, with locals playing cards and arguing over something or other. But we did happen to have the best dinner I've ever had in my life.

Nobody in the restaurant spoke a word of English. Or French, for that matter. So we were helpless captives. One of the waiters recognized us as the Americans they had been told about, so he ushered us to a table and just started bringing food over. Since our friend at the hotel had told them we liked truffles, it was truffles we were served. The first dish was sliced raw beef topped with thinly sliced truffles and olive oil. Then came a pasta dish—ravioli stuffed with truffles and topped with truffle cream. Then came another pasta dish—gnocchi in red-pepper truffle sauce. Then came *another* pasta—ravioli stuffed with roast pheasant and, you guessed it, truffles.

Before we came into the restaurant, Janis had made a point of saying that she wanted to pay for dinner; she hadn't been allowed to pay for anything on the trip so far. My mother agreed to keep her hands off the check, as did I (Norton's only flaw is that he *never* picks up the check, so we didn't bother to clear it with him). However, at this point in the meal, as we realized there was more food still to come, I pointed out to Janis that, with all the truffles we were getting, this meal was likely to cost several million dollars (or several billion lira, as the case may be). That certainly didn't stop us from eating, however. We were then served a guinea hen roasted with truffles—that was the highlight, for me—and then, believe it or not, we were each served a small beefsteak topped with truffles and grated fresh Parmesan cheese. At this point, I thought there was a fifty-fifty chance I was going to explode.

Even Norton had had enough by this time. Still exhausted from his tour of Lucca, he even decided he'd get off his own chair and snuggle up onto my lap for a while. He figured he deserved a soft lap and some petting while we were waiting for dessert.

All during dinner, there was a man sitting at the table behind us. He had a loud, gravelly voice; he sounded as if Lucca Brazi had, some years earlier, removed his vocal chords with a fork. The entire time we were there, he would point over at Norton, pound the table, laugh incredibly loudly, and scream out to the entire restaurant, *"Il gatto! Incredibile!"* This went on for hours.

The incredible *gatto* was now sound asleep on my lap, but the humans were still going. The waiter brought out some chocolate-covered grapes and three round custard-filled doughy pastries, with miniature American flags stuck into them.

Finally, when we were finished stuffing our faces, the owner of the restaurant made an appearance. He sat down with us and we did our best to converse, although there really was a serious language barrier. We got him to understand that my mother worked with some famous chefs back in Los Angeles, and he got all excited, ran back into another room somewhere, then returned with his scrapbook. As we were flipping through it, admiring his various clippings and credentials, we realized that many of the chefs my mother was friendly with had come to study under or work with this guy. Suddenly she was looking at pictures of her L.A. cooking pals, all with their arms around Mr. Truffle. Needless to say, this lent a whole new air of excitement to our evening. Everyone started talking loudly and waving their hands, even though no one had any idea what anyone else was saying. After we'd gone through all the clippings, he took us on a tour of the kitchen and the rest of the restaurant and then introduced us to his mother—who was eighty-three years old and was still the chef for the restaurant. She'd done all the cooking that night—and did all the cooking six nights a week. We learned that it was her father who'd started the restaurant sixty years earlier.

The check came—and it was embarrassingly low after my snide comment; he hardly charged us for anything, much less for the truffles—and with it came a complimentary bottle of *grappa*. Even for us, that was just too much. We told him we couldn't possibly eat or drink one more thing, so our host and new pal wrapped up the bottle and told us to take it back to France, which of course we did.

As we left, we got hugged and kissed by the old mother, and we were hugging and kissing anyone else who got in our way. Norton had revived himself, so he came in for some heavy petting, too. As we stepped out the door, we were told that we—all four of us—would be welcome back whenever we happened to be in the neighborhood.

a cat in sicily (and other places)

One of the things Janis most wanted to do on her year's sabbatical was travel. Unlike me, who left to my own devices would have been content to plop down in Goult and plop up a year later when it was time to leave, Janis wanted to visit as many places and see as many new things as possible.

Having positions that couldn't be more polar opposites, we compromised. We would travel and visit and see as much as we could until I got too cranky and started complaining. At that point, we'd either return to Goult or find a nice, quiet beach somewhere where the most active moment would be turning over from back to stomach to tan another side of the body.

We wound up moving around quite a bit and, of course, wherever we moved, Norton moved. We and he would have it no other way.

One of my fantasies in life is to, one of these days, spend a

201

month or two being a ski bum. I don't actually ski very often or very well, although I can get down a not-too-difficult slope without killing myself. But I enjoy it and it seems like something worth mastering. The idea of paralleling down a mountain at breakneck speed is extraordinarily appealing to me, although I know if I really went at it, there's a good chance I'd wind up in a Swiss emergency room looking a lot like the Boris Karloff version of *The Mummy.*

Norton had been cross-country skiing in Vermont, where I must confess he spent most of the trek on my shoulder, though he did run around in the bushes, following the trail for part of the time. I decided he'd like to see the Alps, so we drove up into the mountains for a weekend.

Janis's idea of fun, in case you were ever in doubt, does not include skiing. It does not, in fact, include any activity where it's possible to break a bone, scrape skin off the body, or ever possibly see one's own blood. But even she was charmed by Aix-les-Bains, on the French side of the Alps.

She got her hopes up as we pulled into town, when she saw there was no snow on the ground. I pointed out to her, however, that the skiing—and thus the snow—was several miles higher. We would stay in Les Bains for two nights, but most of our activities would take place up by the ski slopes.

At this point in the narrative, I would like to interrupt to give a free lesson to everyone reading this book: Don't, under any circumstances, ever try to teach your spouse to ski. It's much, *much* worse than teaching the proper way to drive a stick shift.

I think it sufficient to say that Janis fell down fourteen times in the first three minutes of our lesson. Most of those were directly in front of the ski shop where we rented our equipment. She never even made it to the beginners' slope. Within seconds of her final tumble, her skis were off and she was sitting in the warm restaurant trying to decide which she hated more, skiing or me.

Even Norton deserted me on this occasion. He just wasn't in the mood to frolic in the snow, so he joined Janis for the cat equivalent of a hot toddy.

By the time I'd gotten in my ski time, both girlfriend and cat were, luckily for me, warm and relaxed. They liked the *raclette* dinner I took them to much more than they liked battling nature.

A *raclette* is a very special Alps experience. *Raclette* is a type of cheese that comes in a large brick. When it's served up in the mountains, it's placed on a special *raclette* oven that gets extremely hot and melts the cheese down layer by layer. As it melts, people at the table reach over and use everything from bread to *vinaigred* onions to *cornichons* to tiny baked potatoes to scoop the now-gooey cheese up and eat it. Add some good beer or a cold bottle of white wine, plus a stunning view of the snow-covered Alps, and you've got a memorable dining experience.

Norton was quite pleased with his first *raclette* experience. He was also pleased with the owner of the restaurant, who kept wagging his finger at Norton and enticing him through the swinging door into the kitchen. Every few minutes, we'd hear a "Psssttt" and turn to see the owner, visible through the small porthole in the kitchen door, motioning for the cat to join him. Norton would hop off his chair, disappear for a few moments, then return happily licking his lips.

As our year abroad was drawing to a close, *The Cat Who Went to Paris* began to be published in various countries around the world. Several of those countries wanted Norton to come do publicity.

England was the one country Norton couldn't visit, since they still have that horrendous six-month quarantine for all animals. But at least the Brits could understand the language and most of the references made in the book. The Japanese translator had a few problems.

While we were in Goult, she wrote me the following note:

> *Dear Mr. Gethers,*
>
> *It was my great pleasure to translate your book. I can't believe there is such an amazing cat as Norton. I have been a dog lover and afraid of cats since my childhood, but through the translation of this book, I have changed greatly. Now I can walk up to a cat, say hello, and scratch under his (or her) chin. I am surprised to know how beautiful and elegant the felines are.*
>
> *While translating Norton's story into Japanese, I came across a lot of phrases and a lot of proper nouns which I couldn't understand. I will be very happy if you kindly answer the following questions.*

She then proceeded to list all the things she couldn't understand. By the time I got to the end of the list, I was not only amazed that she liked it, I was shocked she had any idea at all what I was writing about. Plus, when I saw the particular references she was questioning, I became a little worried about my own sensibility.

Her first question was: "Is Eric your older brother or younger brother? I have to know which, because in Japan we use a different word for each of them." (More than anything, this made me happy I was only learning French, not Japanese.) Her next question was: "Tarte tatin. What is this? How do you pronounce these words?" (This also made me happy I was living in France rather than Japan.) The list went on: "P. 20. Willie Davis, Willie Wilson, Willie Mays. Who are they? Please explain about them." "P. 20: Who is Roger 'the Dodger' Staubach? Is 'the Dodger' his nickname?" "Grand High Exalted Wizard. What is this?" "What is kibble? Cat food?" "Ted Bundy. Please explain." "Who are the Seven Santini Brothers?" "Who is John Gotti? A real man or an imaginary one?" "What are the Rams? And why do they stink? Please explain." "What kind of shop is Victoria's Secret?" "What is the Liberace Museum in Las Vegas?" "I do not understand the phrase 'Jack La Lanne's personal hell.' Who is Jack La Lanne?"

It went on, but you get the idea. More than anything else, I wondered if there was any other book ever published that had references to Willie Mays, Ted Bundy, kibble, Victoria's Secret, and the Seven Santini Brothers. Probably not. And that was probably a good thing.

The Dutch had a few problems, too. They didn't know the reference to The Grand High Exalted Wizard either, which, of course, is from "The Honeymooners," from whence Norton derives his memorable moniker. They also didn't know who Laura Petrie or Oscar the Grouch were. They did know who Willie Mays was, which made me feel somewhat better. I never heard from the Italian, German, or Swedish translators, so I assume those countries all watch old Seven Santini Brothers movies and shop mail order at Victoria's Secret.

The Dutch publisher invited us to come up from Provence for the publication in Holland. In Amsterdam— where, several years before, Norton had taken the town by storm when we went there with Polanski—my cat picked up exactly where he left off.

The afternoon we arrived, the publisher, a delightful woman named Hanca Leppink, who ran the firm of Luitingh Sijthoff (don't worry: I can't come close to pronouncing it either), had a pub party for Norton up in her conference room. The entire staff turned up to shake hands (or paws) with *De kat die naar Parijs gin.* The humans all drank champagne and munched on Dutch hors d'oeuvres while the star of the party, a certain Scottish Fold, sat in the center of the room munching on his own special plate of herring while everyone at the company took turns petting him.

After the party, Hanca and a few other people from the office took Janis, Norton, and me out to dinner. Norton, still a bit full from all that raw herring, barely nibbled at his share of the *rijstaffel,* though he enjoyed the evening immensely.

The next two days in Amsterdam were spent being interviewed and photographed by Dutch and Belgian newspapers and magazines. The interviews proved to be remarkably similar to the American interviews we'd done—with one exception. There was one question that all Americans stayed away from. But every single Dutch journalist made a point of bringing this up: They wanted to know what I would do when Norton died.

I was so startled by the question and the topic that the first time I had to give an answer, I fumbled and stumbled through some complete piece of pap. By the third or fourth time this came up, I was at least composed, though I never was able to come up with anything satisfactory, much less glib. Basically, what I said is exactly what I felt: This was something I would have great difficulty dealing with and I didn't think I had to begin dealing with it yet. There was a good chance Norton would live for another ten years, at least. Who knew what would happen in ten years? Who knew if *I'd* be alive in ten years?

To be honest, Norton's death is something I'm not able to think about. I know it happens to the best of us; I've certainly been through it with humans, with those closest to me, those whom I've loved the most. Yet, somehow, it's different with my cat. Maybe it's because there's no formal language with which to directly communicate caring or sorrow. When a parent is old or dying, it's easy (unless you're British) to say the words "I love you." And once those words are said, it makes everything less difficult, even the pain of a final separation. Perhaps that kind of verbal communication assuages guilt. Perhaps it's merely a soothing way to release emotions. But with an animal, words are meaningless. It's actions that count (which, strangely enough since I'm a writer, I prefer. I don't really trust words. They can be used to manipulate too easily). In a sense, there's no way to finalize and communicate grief to an animal. And somehow that makes grief all the more difficult to comprehend and come to grips with.

There's no real point to this diatribe except to say that, after my morbid grilling by the Dutch, I think I've become even more solicitous of Norton. When it does finally come time to say good-bye to him, I want to be sure he knows how much he's meant to me.

I may not be able to *tell* him I love him, but I sure can *show* him.

~~~

Our brief trip to Amsterdam was notable for a few other memorable moments. I don't know whether I'm responsible for this great cultural leap forward, but I do know that the week Norton and I were there promoting our book, "The Honeymooners" made its first ever appearance on Dutch TV. In the television listings, under the heading for 7 P.M. on the channel Nederland 3, it read: *"Honeymooners. Is een in 1955 opgenomen komische Amerikaanse serie over twee echtparen. De opschepperige bus-chauffeur Ralph Kramden en zign vrouw Alice, en hun buren Ed en Trixie Norton."* I have absolutely no idea what that means, but I desperately hope *opgenomen komische* is the Dutch translation for "Raccoon Lodge."

I'd been to Amsterdam for the first time twenty years before. What I mostly remembered from that trip was that hashish was legal and that, if you took the boat trip up and down the canals, you heard the single most annoying phrase in the world over and over and *over* again. On those trips, the tour guides repeat everything in four languages: English, French, German, and Dutch. So, near the beginning of the tour, when they tell you the history of how Amsterdam got its name, you hear this, in a lilting, lovely accented English: "First the town was built around the Amstel River. And the dams were what made the river function. So you see? Amstel . . . dam . . . Ams*tel*dam . . . *Amster*dam!" Then, once the English version is finished, a couple of minutes later, you hear the guide, blabbing away in German. You don't understand anything you hear until the guide comes to the phrase "Amstel . . . dam . . . Ams*tel*dam . . . *Amster*dam!" A few minutes after that, the French begins and you can maybe pick out one or two phrases, and then comes "Amstel . . . dam . . . Ams*tel*dam . . . *Amster*dam!" And there's still one more to go. There's some guttural Dutch, then some more guttural Dutch, then even more guttural Dutch, then, that's right: "Amstel . . . dam . . . Ams*tel*-

dam . . . *Amster*dam!" Believe me, this is not something you can get out of your mind easily. Twenty years later, if someone orders an Amstel Light, I find myself going, "Amstel . . . light . . . Amstellight . . . Amster Light!"

I'm almost over the fixation now, and I suppose I should get serious psychiatric help, but I did refuse to take another canal tour with Norton and Janis. I didn't want to be repeating that phrase over and over to myself when I'm eighty years old and living in the home for aged cat owners.

One thing I did revisit while in Amsterdam was the Anne Frank house.

Janis and I walked to the famed hiding place with Norton on my shoulder. Two blocks away, Janis suddenly went sprawling in the middle of the street. I helped her up, concerned but certainly not overly concerned, figuring she'd merely tripped. But when she was back on her feet, tears were streaming down her cheeks and she grabbed me, bordering on hysteria. Astonished, I asked her what the hell was going on.

"You don't understand," she sobbed. "I sprain my ankle almost every week! My ankles are so weak I can hardly walk and it hurts so *much!*"

"Don't cry," I tried to soothe. "It's not the worst thing in the world."

That only made her sob harder. "It *is* the worst thing in the world. I can't walk without hurting myself! And I look like an idiot, falling down all the time! *What could be worse!!!*"

"Well," I said slowly, holding her in my arms and thinking about where we were headed, "how about being forced to hide in an attic for three years and then being killed by Nazis?"

That ended the ankle problem and any ensuing complaints. We then walked—slowly—to the museum and, with a subdued cat, saw where the tragic story had all transpired.

Afterward, we walked back to our hotel in silence—it's almost impossible to talk after being enveloped by the sadness of that house. Janis didn't mention her ankle and, for the first time in months, Norton didn't meow repeatedly to let me know it was past his feeding time.

~~~

Our last major trip of the year was to Sicily, a place I'd desperately wanted to visit after sitting through *Godfather I* and *II* forty-seven times each.

We were particularly excited about going. It seemed more exotic than our other travels yet not at all intimidating. It promised to be luxurious yet still mysterious. There was Italian food, but even better than normal because it was *garlicy* Italian food. And we knew Norton would be accepted. He'd seen *The Godfather* at least as many times as I had.

Getting there was your basic nightmare, unfortunately. This is the worst thing about traveling with a cat: If a plane's late, a person can relax in the bar, go to the bathroom, do whatever he wants. But it's extremely difficult for a cat to cope when takeoff is delayed by an hour or two. I do everything possible to keep things under control for Norton. He has access to his litter box until the last possible moment. He's free to roam around at all times except for when airline officials tell me he must be in his traveling kennel. And, of course, Norton is an experienced traveler, so he rarely panics. But it's not fair to keep a cat away from a litter box too long (even Norton has his limits), and though I try to make traveling as comfortable as possible for him, it has to be faced that he must go through some inconveniences if he wants to come along.

The plane leaving for Rome was an hour and a half late. Luckily the plane was fairly empty and, having learned my lesson from a couple of accidents early in our traveling experiences, I brought a portable litter box on board. I didn't fill it up with litter—that would have been a little much—but I did unfold it and put it under the seat in front of me. Every twenty minutes or so, I'd put Norton in the box until he got the urge to use it. Then I was able to get rid of the box in the bathroom—and no one on the plane was ever bothered.

The airline officials in Italy are even more relaxed than in France. For both takeoffs and landings (from Marseille to Rome, then from Rome to Catania in Sicily), the stewards let Norton sit calmly on my lap. I think he reminded them a little bit of Marcello Mastroianni, so they just decided to leave him be.

Supposedly, our hotel was about an hour's drive from the Catania airport. There was one small problem, however: It's not possible to get *out* of Catania. We picked up our rental car (and immediately put a litter box *with* litter on the floor in the back), took a look at our instructions, drove away—and got hopelessly lost. We were told to leave the airport and look for signs that lead to the autostrade, then take that in the direction of the town of Enna. We left the airport—and there were no signs. Not one. Not even a stop sign at the intersection. We took a guess and made a right, heading down a road that looked like something out of *Mad Max*. After fifteen minutes of aimless driving through slums

and totally deserted, burnt-out areas, we stopped and mo-
tioned to a pedestrian. "Autostrade?" we said pathetically.
"Enna?"

We got directions promptly (and loudly)—but they were
the wrong directions. After another bewildering fifteen
minutes, we stopped and asked somebody else. This person
shook his head gravely, started doing "tsk tsk" with his
tongue, and told us we were lost. Thanks a lot, pal. He then
gave us long, complicated *new* directions, which also
proved to be completely wrong. Eventually we struck out
on our own again and found the autostrade, although we
never saw a sign that said anything even remotely resem-
bling ENNA. However, we did see something that pointed
us toward Messina, which the map showed was approximately the right direction. The miracle of it all was that we
were told it would take us an hour to get to Taormina,
where we were staying, and when we pulled up to our
hotel, the trip had taken exactly an hour. The moral of that
story is that normal directions in Sicily seem to be, "First
you pull out of the airport. Then you get lost for half an
hour and feel like an idiot . . ."

I don't want to turn this section into a travelogue. Let's
just leave it that Norton did all the usual touring. He went
to the Villa Romana, near the Piazza Armerina, which has
incredible Roman tiles (Janis liked the ones of the birds
with bright plumage; I preferred the bikini-clad women
dancing arm in arm). We went up to Castlemodo, a little
town that overlooks what seems to be the entire world.
Norton got lugged to Siracusa, which once was the center
of the world and, judging from everything I've seen, probably should be again. He went with us to Noto, an eighteenth-century village which is entirely gold-hewed. Even
the white wine has a bronze tint to it. He also went to

Agricento and the extraordinary Valley of the Temples and to the town of Sciacca, a city of thermal baths (I'm sure this doesn't need to be said, but yes, I did drive Janis crazy doing a lot of Sciacca Therapy jokes). We had dinner one night in a total nontouristy town called Forza d'Agro. We ate at a small café as farmers walked by, carrying on their heads baskets of grain and fruit and even chickens, on their way home from the fields. Wild cats kept coming up to our table to beg for food, which I think made Norton feel a little guilty. Also somewhat thankful that he was with us, rather than out on his own.

The only place Norton didn't go with us was to see Mount Etna—while it was exploding. We went at night and it was an awesome sight, beautiful and terrible at the same time. Everywhere we looked there was molten red lava flowing down the mountain toward small besieged villages. I figured Norton was better off in the hotel. I didn't know if he'd be feeling adventurous, but I didn't particularly want to deal with having a Scottish Fold Red Adair on my hands.

Of the places we stayed, Norton much preferred Taormina. We stayed in a fifteenth-century castle that stood on a cliff, looming several hundred feet over the sea. And when I say looming, I mean *looming*. The first thing Norton did when we checked in was to dash out onto our balcony and go racing—much too fast to do my heart much good—across the very narrow ledge, the entire length of the hotel. Practically every minute we were in our room, Norton spent on that ledge, staring out over the water far below. If he wasn't there, he was outside by the pool, which was also located high above the sea. He liked it there, too, mostly because the waitresses would bring him little strips of chicken while he sat on his chaise longue.

The highlight of our Sicilian trip, without question, was

discovering an inn and restaurant in the middle of nowhere (or near the town of Gangivecchia, to be more precise, absolutely smack dab in the middle of the island). The restaurant is called The ex-Convento di Gangivecchia. It's called that, cleverly enough, because it's an ex-convent, dating from the thirteenth century.

It's a giant and magnificent structure, over forty rooms, surrounded by two hundred acres of gardens and farmland—everything served there is grown or slaughtered there, too—and it's run by two women, a mother and daughter, the Baroness Wanda Tornabene and Giovanna Tornabene. We made so many pleasurable groaning noises while we were eating the asparagus fritter, the fresh *tapenade,* the homemade gnocchi in eggplant and tomato sauce, and the homemade cannolis and hot lemon-curd fritters, that the Baroness came over to our table to talk (I think she was just happy to get us to stop eating). She admired Norton right off, which endeared her to us, and told us that the last such distinguished visitor at the ex-Convento was Prince Charles. Personally, I think Norton could have held on to Di if he'd had the chance, so I didn't think much of the comparison, but I thanked her for the compliment anyway.

Despite the fact that the ex-Convento was three hours from anywhere a normal person might be in Sicily, the three of us drove back there four days later—when I told Janis that I might kill someone if I saw another Roman temple. Since it was his second visit, Norton felt right at home and made himself comfortable while he explored various rooms supposedly off-limits to customers. But the Tornabenes didn't mind. In fact, when we left, we discovered there was no check.

They felt honored to be able to treat Signore Norton to a good lunch, they said.

Touched, I told them that Signore Norton was equally honored. I, however, was happy the next day when it was time for the gray Signore to return to France. If he spent much more time in Sicily, I believe his little folded ears might just have been overwhelmed by his ever-larger swelled head.

a cat in goult

On New Year's Day of last year, our French friends gave us a present: They provided us with the most wonderful day I've ever spent. In so many ways it's what our entire year was all about.

Our friends in Goult had a tradition. For ten years, they'd hiked up into the mountains on New Year's Day. The hike was a relatively easy one, beginning just above the town of St. Saturnin d'Apt. Each year, they started at the same spot and hiked about an hour until they reached an old deserted stone village, abandoned over a hundred years ago when the town's water supply ran out. Everyone who hiked had to bring some form of good food or drink; when they arrived at the abandoned village—called Travignon—everyone then ate and drank, napped in the sun, celebrated another year of good living, wished for a new year with more of the same, then hiked back home, happy, tired, a

217

little bit drunk, and more than a little bit filled with good cheer.

A few weeks before Christmas, Janis, Norton, and I were invited on their hike. Touched and honored, we agreed immediately, though we warned them that two other Americans would also be with us—that was the week Norm and Esther came visiting. No problem, we were told. We were official Goultoise now and we could invite whomever we wanted.

The day before New Year's Day was cold and wintry. The day after New Year's Day was even colder and rainy. But our *bons amis* had assured us that the weather for their New Year's hike was always perfect—and when we awoke that day, the sun was shining down and the sky was blue and clear.

I had crudités and wine stuffed into my backpack and a curious cat stuffed into my shoulder bag as we hiked up into the hills. We all bounced along, chattering in bizaare pigeon-English and pseudo-French, everyone being ultrasensitive to everyone else's inability to communicate properly. We took in the glory of the countryside until we reached Travignon, situated at the top of the mountain. It was a kind of hippie camp now. In the structures that still had roofs, there were mattresses, tattered sleeping bags, and crude tables made out of large rocks. There was also a nice tradition: In some of the ruins, there were full bottles of wine, left by the last person to sleep there, waiting to greet the next camper.

The sun was shining and warm (the official weather word on Provence from the locals: a cold climate with a hot sun—and that's the perfect description) and it was now time to eat. Blankets were spread on the ground. Cheese and fruit and bread were spread out; wine was opened. We gathered kindling to build a campfire, on which was cooked delicious homemade sausages.

After lunch, some of the group went off hiking and prowling. Two American pseudo-Goultoise lay down on a large, surprisingly comfortable rock and took naps in the sun. The smallest, grayest, flattest-earred member of the hike did his best to poke through the campfire and eat as many leftover sausage bits as he could find before joining his dad in the midday snooze.

Years of tradition broke on the hike back. We all realized we weren't ready for the day to end, so we went back to one of the hikers' houses to prolong the warmth and good cheer. We ate pasta and sat around until one in the morning listening to our friend Jean-Guy, a musician, play the guitar and sing his own, romantic compositions. Norton was having such a good time, I'm sure that if only Jean-Guy knew any tunes in English, one member of the hike would have happily meowed out the words to "Michael Row the Boat Ashore."

By the time we made it back to our house, the day had become a dreamlike experience. Friendships were cemented, new traditions were established, new levels of communication had been reached. Sometimes when I'm lecturing about the wonders of my cat, I do feel a little guilty and feel as if I should add a P.S., which I will add here, that occasionally people—even relative strangers— can also provide an awful lot of the good things in life.

There is a New Year's superstition in France. It is believed that the first twelve days of the year are crucial to one's happiness. If the first day is a good one, you will have a good month of January. If day two goes well, so will February. If day three is fine, March will be a lucky month, and so on. I don't remember all the details of our first twelve days of last year, but it's certain we were living under a lucky star. Or perhaps it's easier to make your own luck when surrounded by true friends, Monsieur Bonnelly's wine, and a cat who appreciates the splendor and glory of the hot Provençal sun.

~~~

As all good things must, our year abroad did end.

Duty, not to mention the need to make a living, called.

In our last weeks, we went from town to town—from nontouristy Jucas and Murs to the magnificent red cliffs of Roussillon to the chilly ruins of Oppede-le-vieux—soaking it all in, trying to sere into our brains not only the magnificent sights but the European attitude and the feeling of appreciation for life which we hoped to carry back to America. We lunched in the wonderful villages of Manosque, stuffed ourselves with desserts from the *pâtisserie* in Cabrieres, toured the beauteous St.-Rémy and the rest of the region known as Les Alpilles, and often just sat in our house in Goult, sipping a glass of cold rosé wine and marveling at the splendor we could find in our own backyard.

Our last night in Goult, our friend Anne had a small dinner party. Just our close circle of French friends (though one woman, Anette, was Swedish, she was considered honorary French, having lived in Goult for years).

We sat around Anne's dining table—Janis, Norton, myself, our new friends—talking easily and eating well, of course, and, naturally, drinking a lot of good red wine. And during the evening, our sense of sadness lifted. We somehow knew we'd be back. Or these new people in our lives would visit us in New York. Or that, even if we never saw them again, they'd all somehow be with us for the rest of our lives.

At midnight, we knew it was finally time to say good-bye. Everyone kissed and hugged and exchanged small gifts of farewell and of thanks. Then Janis, Norton, and I strolled the two or three streets back to our house. When we rounded the corner across from the restaurant Le Tonneau, walking along the front of Goult's thousand-year-old castle, we found ourselves at the very spot of the dread outdoor bird cage. But the birds were not there; for some reason they'd been taken inside. Norton, not believing his good fortune but wanting to take advantage of it, hesitated, then walked to the front door of the house and sniffed cautiously. Proudly, he turned toward us and took one strutting step forward. At that moment, we heard the loud chirp of a bird from somewhere within the house. A final farewell.

Norton led the way, of course, but Janis and I sprinted after him the best we could, running and laughing—and meowing—all the way back to our three-hundred-year-old home.

And the next morning, we were still laughing—and meowing—as we left Goult and headed back to America.

PART THREE

a
cat
returns

a cat in new york

11

Janis and I returned home wondering exactly how we were going to resume our previous lives. Our careers were up in the air—her sabbatical was over and she had to find out what, if indeed any, job was waiting for her; I had to decide whether or not to return to corporate life—as were our living arrangements, our relationship, and all sorts of other loose ends.

Norton had none of those questions to resolve. He returned to find himself a changed man (I know that's not exactly right, but it sounds a lot better than "a changed cat"). He returned to find himself a celebrity.

Soon after arriving back in New York, Norton and I were on the road again, traveling to Los Angeles for business and venturing around the country for the paperback publicity tour for *The Cat Who Went to Paris*.

The first indication I had that, in the year we were away, fame had found a certain Scottish Fold, came in Boston.

Norton and I were sitting in the lobby of the Boston Four
Seasons, being interviewed by a reporter for a Boston
paper. All of a sudden, three women walked by—a fiftyish
mother and her two thirtyish daughters—and the mother
stopped short, turned, and stared straight at us.

"Oh my god!" she said slowly. "Is that *him?*"

For one brief, shining moment, I, of course, thought she
was referring to me. Yeah, *right.*

"Is that *Norton?!*" she squealed and came rushing over to
pet him.

When I acknowledged that the creature now on his back
and purring loudly was indeed Norton, she called her
two daughters over to meet him. It turns out she'd read
the book a year earlier and, since she traveled a lot, had
kept her eye open for you-know-who whenever she was on
the road.

"I *knew* I'd run into him one of these days," she gushed.
"Do you think he'd ever want to come up and visit us on
the Cape?"

This was by no means his only brush with Fold groupies.
When I—excuse me, we—appeared at Books & Company
in Dayton, Ohio, one woman came up and shyly told me
she'd driven over a hundred miles just to meet Norton.
Since she'd come so far, I introduced the two of them and
left them alone for several minutes. When their chat was
over, the woman didn't seem at all disappointed. In fact, she
had a big smile on her face. I have no idea what they
discussed and decided I was better off not knowing.

In Detroit he was recognized in the airport. As we were
boarding the plane, a woman came over and asked whether
that was that strange cat who went to Paris. When I said yes,
she asked if she could have his autograph. I tried to explain
to her that even though he was a very smart cat, he couldn't

actually hold a pen and write. So she wouldn't be too disillusioned, I told her I was sure he could spell his name, but the problem was a lack of opposable thumbs. That seemed to satisfy her.

In Los Angeles, a bellman at the Four Seasons told me a great story. He said he was helping two women up to their rooms and he overheard them talking about a book they'd read about a most amazing cat.

"Ladies," he said to them. "Excuse me for kibitzing your conversation, but are you talking about Norton Gethers?"

Astonished, they said that they were. "But how did you know?" one of them asked him.

"Because he stays here," the bellman told the women. "I know him. This is Norton's hotel of choice."

Norton and I were in L.A. that trip to talk about selling the movie rights to our book. Initially, quite a few producers and directors were interested. There was a lot of talk about Mel Gibson as me (a natural, I figured) and Michelle Pfeiffer as Janis (a natural, she figured). Norton was tough casting—I thought maybe they'd get a dog who was an impressionist—but that wasn't really my problem. We narrowed the list down to five producers, then those five took it to their respective film studios. That's when we ran into a bit of trouble.

The first executive called me from 20th Century-Fox. "I like it," she said. "But I think it's a little soft. Explain to me how you'd turn it into a movie." So I did. I went through Act One, Act Two, and Act Three. I told how I'd develop the characters and I told exactly what role the cat would play. "I still like it," she said when I was finished. "But I still think it's a little soft. Is it possible that we can add some sort of thriller element?"

"Like a Cat-Meets-Clint-Eastwood-kind-of-a-thing?" I said. *"Dirty Norton?"*

"That's interesting," she said. "That's a very interesting way to go."

"Not for me," I told her and hung up.

The next executive I had to go through was at Warner Brothers. She, too, felt it was a little soft for a movie. So I went through the same pitch, told her how it would work, and she said, "I like it. But do you think it would be possible to have the cat talk?"

"You mean like *Look Who's Meowing?*"

"Exactly," she said.

"I'm hanging up now," I said.

The third person worked at the Imagine film studio. We went through the usual exchange—Her: too soft; Me: here's how to do it—and then when I was all finished, we had this memorable exchange:

"I love it," she told me. "I really do." (Important Aside: The phrase "I love it" is totally meaningless. Studio executives want you to like them, so they never tell you face-to-face that they think anything is bad. Afterward, they just refuse to take your phone calls, so you get the hint that they don't want to do your project.) "But," she went on, "you have to help me with one thing."

"Anything," I promised.

"What do I do when my boss comes into my office and says, 'How is this different from *Turner and Hootch?*' "

"You mean the Tom Hanks police thriller about a cop and his dog?" I asked.

"Uh-huh," she said.

"Welllll . . . that's a tough one," I agreed. "How about telling him this *isn't* a police thriller, there's *no* cop and *no* dog?"

"I don't know if that'll do it," she said.

That's when I called my agent and told him I didn't want to have any more conversations about turning the book into a movie. So Norton wouldn't ever get his paw prints in front of Mann's Chinese Theater—we could live with that. At least I could.

This isn't to say that he was ignored by his adoring public. I would guess that, over time, we've received a thousand letters from people who've read *The Cat Who Went to Paris.* Every so often, someone mentions that they liked the book. Mostly, people ask questions about Norton. Or just praise him. Some people send him presents. Norton has received his own Feline Passport (a popular new product, so I'm told), he got a self-published book of poetry that was dedicated to him, and he was sent several inspirational poems, framed quite nicely. One woman sent him a package that included a couple of cans of Pounce, a lovely salt shaker (don't ask me—I just report the facts!), a Christmas tree ornament, and a photo of her car, which she thought he'd be interested in seeing.

Many people send photos of their cats. I'm glad to report they usually preface these with the words "Dear Norton, I know my little [fill in the blank: Daffodil, Sarge, or Ezekial] isn't as handsome as you are but . . ."

Most of the letters are actually wonderful. A lot of people were moved by the story of the death of my father and wanted to let me know that by sharing my grief I'd helped them with theirs. Many letters began with phrases like "Dear Peter and Norton, Excuse the familiarity of the greeting, but I feel like I know you both so well now. You seem like old pals." Many letters, amazingly enough, were simply addressed to Norton, Sag Harbor, New York. Don't ask me how the post office knew to deliver them, but they arrived.

Norton and I got letters from ninety-year-old people letting me know that my book inspired them to get one last cat before they died; women who sent semi-suggestive photos or suggestions along with invitations to visit anytime (my favorite enticement was from one woman who ended her letter with: "I keep a can of Pounce handy at all times. One in the kitchen, one in the bedroom. You're welcome to use either one." I don't know about you, but a can of shrimp Pounce by the bed turns *me* on!); letters from people with AIDS who told me their cats provided them with enormous solace and comfort; and one extraordinarily moving call from a woman who had a retarded daughter and wanted to tell me that the only thing that made her daughter smile was when she looked at the photo of Norton on the cover of our book.

Some people wrote eloquently of being touched by my relationship with Norton and by his unique personality. Others wrote simply to tell me that my feelings about Norton made them realize how much they loved their own cats.

I got several angry letters and calls, too. Several people worried that I placed my cat in too many dangerous situations (which I don't—honest), and one man wrote me an extremely nasty letter, telling me that just because my life was so interesting was no reason to write a book shoving his face in the fact that his life was so boring.

The ASPCA got in touch with me. They were putting out a book of photographs of famous animals. Would Norton agree to be included? It was for a good cause, so I agreed. Then they called back and said that the person in charge of the project had just read my book—and he was shocked to find that I let Norton eat ice cream and jelly doughnuts. He found that so offensive, he wouldn't allow Norton to be associated with his work.

And people wonder why organizations have trouble getting donations.

My two very favorite letters came from young girls (get your mind out of the gutter!).

One was from a thirteen-year-old in Greater Manchester, England. After telling me that *The Cat Who Went to Paris* was her favorite book ever, she added such gems as: "We have a cat named Floyd and he is just like Norton except (1) he has blue eyes, (2) he is not a Scottish Fold and (3) he is not very smart." Other than that, exactly alike. My English fan also told me that she "ranked the book as one of the greatest modern books ever written." Ah, yes. *The Brothers Karamazov, The Great Gatsby,* and *The Cat Who Went to Paris,* not necessarily in that order.

The best of them all, however, came from an eleven-year-old girl in Colorado. Here's how her letter began: "Dear Mr. Gethers, I just want to tell you that your book is one of the *absolute best* books I have *ever* read (and believe me I read almost everything). I'm in love with Norton!" She also had this to say, which I liked quite a lot: "To tell you the truth, when I first got your book (for Christmas) I thought it was going to be another hummdrumm book (like us kids so commonly get). But it definitely wasn't!" What made her letter so memorable, however, was her spelling. Among the misspelled words: seems (seams), believe (belive), commonly (comenly), commonly (comonly), definitely (defenetly), wasn't (wasen't), perfect (perfict), writing (writeing), and please (pelease). At the end, she added these two wonderful addendums: "P.S. I admire your work because I want to be a author also and I hope I can be as good as you. P.P.S. Sorry my spelling isn't grate."

~~~

One of the most amazing side effects of writing about my
cat is how interested people are in Norton. They've taken
to him as if he's a member of their own family. The nice
thing is, people seem to appreciate him. They "get" what
it is that makes him so special. Another amazing thing to me
is how interested people became in *my* life. It's a strange
sensation to open yourself up to a hundred thousand people
or so, telling very personal stories about everything from
idiotically talking aloud to a cat to coping with the death of
a parent. But all of a sudden, I find that Norton and I have
this kind of odd (sometimes very odd!) extended family all
over the country. All over the world, in fact. When we're
on the road or via letters or even in the occasional stray
phone call, people tend to want answers to the same questions. I think it might not be a bad idea to answer them all
here. Not only will this save you the twenty-nine cents for
a stamp, it'll keep me from losing my voice on the next tour.

The single most common question—usually asked by
women with thirty-year-old unmarried daughters—is: "Are
you and Janis married yet?" The answer is no. We lived
together for the year we were in France and, except for the
several moments per week when we wanted to kill each
other (especially when she refuses to put the open milk back
in the refrigerator), we did okay. But I don't seem to be the
marrying (or even the living together) kind and neither
does she. We're also both children of the sixties and we
share the same view of marriage: It's only a piece of paper
and a relationship doesn't have to be made legal for it to be
a good one. To top that all off (since you're so nosy), and
I realize this is a character flaw, I figure there is a reasonable

chance I'll one day meet either Sarah Jessica Parker, Michelle Pfeiffer, Katie Couric, Uma Thurman, or Sandra Day O'Connor (okay, okay, I don't *really* think she belongs on this list of sexy women, but I don't want people to think I'm shallow) and if I do, I just don't think I could bring myself to say the words "Hi. Meet the wife."

The second most asked question: "How old is Norton?" Here are all of his vital statistics: By the time this book comes out, he will be ten years old. I'm expecting him to be around at least ten more years (and every time I see an item in a newspaper or magazine about a twenty-two-year-old cat, I make sure I read it aloud to him). He weighs nine and a half pounds, is still pretty trim, is in excellent health (he's been sick twice that I can think of, both times with a touch of the flu), and yes, he does like traveling with me. I am starting to think of getting another cat. I think it would be good for him; it would help keep him young. But I'm still too selfish to do so. Traveling with two cats would be too difficult. Perhaps in another few years, when Norton really starts to slow down and traveling becomes less fun for him.

In descending order, these are the other questions I'm usually bombarded with:

3. *Do cats need passports?* No. When traveling internationally, all they need is a health certificate. They need to have their shots within a week of leaving for Europe—and be sure to keep the record because, to return to America, you have to prove that those shots were received within a year of your return. Any vet knows exactly what shots to give and what papers are needed.

4. *How's your mom?* She's great. I just threw her a surprise seventieth birthday party at Spago (Norton didn't go but he

did send a telegram). She's writing two new cookbooks, travels constantly, is so busy it's hard to get her to sit still for more than two minutes, and generally is quite happy.

5. *Will you publish my cat book?* No.

6. *Will you read my cat book?* Not unless I have to.

7. *Do cats get jet lag?* Think about it. Cats sleep *all* the time. They're not awake long enough to get jet lag!

8. *Why won't my cat act like Norton?* I have no idea. Do you talk to him constantly, pet him incessantly, give him whatever he wants whenever he wants it, and pamper him at first-class hotels all around the world? This may have something to do with it.

9. *Is* The Cat Who Went to Paris *ever going to be a movie? And is Norton going to play himself?* Believe it or not, after the nightmare of trying to sell the book when it first came out, it looks like things worked out after all. The book has been bought by Paramount and the screenplay is in the works. Norton is definitely *not* going to play himself. That's where I drew the line and demanded a stunt cat. However, we did have to go to L.A. recently for a movie pow-wow. Norton and I went onto the studio back lot for our meeting. (The best thing about going to the Paramount back lot are the names of the buildings. You can sit around a conference table in the Bob Hope Building or stroll by the Edith Head Wardrobe Building. If you prefer, you can also rendezvous at the Ernst Lubitsch Annex, at the corner of Rudolph Valentino Place, in the Mary Pickford Wing, or my favorite—and this is where I got to have my meeting—in the Jerry Lewis Building.) We met with the studio executive in charge of the project and the producers of the film. When we walked in, I think they were all a little nervous that Norton would turn out to be somewhat of a letdown. But, as usual, he was anything but. He sat on the couch next to

me for the first part of the meeting, then as he got a little bored hearing all the stories about his life repeated for the umpteenth time, he began to explore. First he sized up the producer's gigantic office, sniffing at the various cupboards, shelves, and tables. Then he hopped up onto the desk and snooped around there, probably trying to catch a glimpse of the contract to see if he had script approval. Then, while we story-conferenced the movie, Norton went out into the hallway and introduced himself to the various secretaries and story editors in their nearby offices. By the time he came back, the script was ready to be written and I think the Paramount executive was thinking of starring Norton in a remake of *Gone With the Wind.* The producer also had a vision of screening the movie, if it's actually made, at the White House. I think he figures we can get a good quote from Socks. My hope is merely that Norton is the first cat invited to a state dinner. Or that he receives some kind of official post (even if it's only a Scratching Post).

10. *Will you write another book about Norton?* No. I think this is it. It's time for me to reclaim my own life as a human being able to stand on my own two feet (or nearly) and to let my cat return to his anonymous, if still extraordinary, ways.

The first book I wrote about Norton ended with the death of my father. Luckily for me, this book does not end with anything nearly so dramatic or traumatic. However, that doesn't mean that life has and will continue to sail a smooth course.

The Cat Who Went to Paris ended with everyone living happily ever after. But, of course, nobody *really* lives happily ever after. Things happen.

Things change.

That's what makes life interesting, if not always sane.

But, to steal from a fairly respectable poetic voice, most things change with a whimper rather than a bang.

My father's been dead three and a half years now and the pain has certainly subsided, but it's a very strange thing: His death has left me with a perpetual sadness. There is a great poem by Gerard Manley Hopkins called "Margaret Are You Grieving?" It's ostensibly about the grief one feels for a loved one who dies, but it's *really* about the fact that what we're feeling is grief for *ourselves.* That what we're all crying about is our own mortality. While I can honestly say I miss my dad every single day in all sorts of little ways—I constantly think how he would have loved a particular movie or book, or how I'd like to get his opinion on something, or how happy he'd have been that Clinton won the election—I know that some of that sadness I'm feeling is for myself. I remember how upset I was when my grandfather died. Then, of course, the pain of my father's death is still a wound, perhaps not so raw anymore but certainly still tender. And then I think, Uh-oh—guess who's next in line?

So, happily, there are no recent deaths to deal with these days, but there is still grief nonetheless. I find myself crying at movies I never would have cried at in the past. Every so often, I'll even find myself crying at bad sitcoms that deal with the subject of loss (and believe me, something's a little screwy when you cry at the rerun of "Family Ties" when Alex goes off to college). There's nothing to do about this. It doesn't affect my life. I have as much fun as I've always had. I laugh just as much as always. It's just that, as one gets older, life gets slightly and irreversibly sadder.

Relationships change, too.

I am, of course, still crazy about my mom. She's as cool

as a mother can be. But, though she's coping wonderfully well with widowhood, she's more nervous about things than she used to be. She spent her whole life taking care of my father. Now there's a void: She needs something and someone else to take care of. I find I'm a lot less patient around her, that I get irritated over practically nothing. This has nothing to do with her. She's still great. It has everything to do with my reaction to the fact that she, too, is getting older and isn't—and couldn't be—the same person she was in the past.

I guess I don't like when things change, although I have yet to discover any way to stop them from doing so.

My brother, Eric—the one who's responsible for giving me Norton—and I don't speak anymore. I thought he was screwing up his life and made the mistake of telling him so, in no uncertain terms. He was equally certain I was wrong. Also that it was none of my business, which in retrospect is hard to argue with. So in a particularly painful conversation, he made it clear that, though at one point when we were younger we were very, very friendly, our lives are no longer entwined.

I've come from a family that was extremely close and loving. And we've been close my entire life. That foundation has always been a big part of my identity. But somehow, inexorably it seems, that family and foundation has eroded. The family no longer exists. It's gone, and that is a change most difficult and painful to adjust to.

Friendships, too, alter themselves. It was interesting to see the reactions when Janis and I left for France. Many of my relationships are professional ones. As a publisher, I buy books from agents, I work closely with authors. Once I stepped down as the head of a company, it was extraordinary to see which agents stopped calling because they decided I was no longer useful, and which authors suddenly realized there might be someone who could be a more beneficial dinner companion. Some people, I think, were resentful that I was actually trying to make my life better. Some didn't give it nearly that much thought and simply moved on to someone else who could help them more.

Even more personal friendships went through changes. Some very close friends resented our leaving, didn't understand why we'd want new friendships and new experiences. They felt that our leaving was some form of rejection. So, much to my surprise, certain relationships were altered, some subtly, some not, for reasons that were beyond my control as well as my comprehension.

One big change, of my own doing, is that I have made my escape from corporate life a long-lasting one. Recently, I was offered the chance to get back on the publishing fast track and run a very large company. This would have meant quite a bit of prestige and more money than I'd ever thought I'd make. But after an agonizing week of worrying about my future and dreaming of a large house in Provence that would now be affordable, I turned the job down. I decided to follow my cat on this one and stay as independent as possible. I may regret it—and already have, on occasion—but when I finally rejected the offer, it was as if a five-hundred-pound weight was lifted from my back. This is one instance where change might be for the better.

Janis and I haven't changed very much. We still have our separate apartments and our separate lives, yet we still have our life together. We both seem to like it this way. Is it permanent? Is it unchangeable? I don't have the foggiest. But we've been through too much together and care about each other way too much to even conceive of anything else. I like our chances.

However, as life shows us over and over again, things do change.

Except for one.

I've spent a lot of time thinking about what it is that makes cats and our relationships to cats so special. Yes, they are extraordinary in their wisdom and their independence and their beauty. Yes, they provide comfort and company and, of course, fun. But it's more than that. I think cats provide permanence.

Cats don't change.

Certainly they get older and certainly they die, but while they're here they are what they are and that's *all* that they are.

Yes, Norton has a tiny touch of arthritis now and can't jump quite as nimbly onto the kitchen cabinet as he used to. And yes, occasionally he will not make the jump at all because he doesn't think he'll make it—which pretty near breaks my heart. And I think he sleeps a bit more than usual and he's no longer quite so eager to go on walks with me—he'd rather stay home and conserve his energy.

But he *is* under my cheek every morning when I wake up.

He meows for breakfast every single day the moment I swing out of bed and my feet touch the floor.

When I come home at night, he's waiting by the front door as soon as my key turns the lock.

When I'm home working, I know that all I have to do is turn slightly to my left and he'll be stretched out on the back of the couch, basking in any sun that might be streaming through the living-room window.

There is absolutely nothing I could do—or ever would do—that could stop him from loving me. And vice versa. There is not much else in life you can say that about.

I'm not old and neither is he, but we're getting older. Just recently I turned forty and Norton turned ten. To celebrate, Janis and I went to New Orleans with some of our closest and dearest friends. We ate *beignets* and oyster po' boys and obscene amounts of crayfish and drank a whole bunch of spicy Cajun martinis and celebrated what's been a pretty damn good life, which is going to, I hope, get even better. We stayed at a beautiful small hotel in the French Quarter called The Lamothe House. When I called to make the reservation, I asked the manager, whose name was Brant, if I could bring my cat.

"I'm terribly sorry," he told me, "but we don't allow pets."

"See, it's my birthday," I started to explain. "And Norton, my cat, kind of goes everywhere I go and this is going to be a big celebration and—"

"Your cat's *Norton?*" Brant asked over the phone.

"Yes," I said, a little taken aback.

"Oh, Norton can come," he then told me matter-of-factly. "Norton's different."

So Norton came. He basked in the sun in the hotel's courtyard, got powdered sugar all over himself eating *beignets* at Café du Monde, charmed the hotel maid, and generally had a good time as we both eased into the next stage of our lives.

And while the older I get, it seems the less I know, I *do* know one thing: For the next important day of my life, whatever and wherever it is, Norton will be there also—to celebrate, to participate, to do whatever it is he decides to do. But he'll be there.

That will never change.

afterword

Janis and I learned all sorts of things from our year living in France.

We learned about wine. We learned how to cook and how to speak a different language. We learned how to balance work with life. We learned how to put a lot of different things in perspective.

Norton learned something, too, which we just discovered.

In our house in Sag Harbor, our bedroom door locks in two ways. It's really two doors that close and meet in the middle of the doorway. On one of them there's a small hook, waist-high, that flips over and catches onto the other door, keeping the doors closed but somewhat flimsily. Then, on the bottom of one of the doors is a latch that slips down and fits into a notch in the floor. This secures both doors as well as our privacy.

We don't usually lock or even close the bedroom door

except when we have overnight guests, because our second bedroom is very nearby. I don't mind being behind closed doors and neither does Janis. Norton, however, doesn't care for it one iota.

He must have a touch of claustrophobia. He almost always spends the entire night in bed with us, but I guess he likes it to be his option because as soon as the door is locked, Norton hops out of bed and decides he has to escape the confines of the room. This is one of the few times in his life he doesn't get his way. When the door's locked, it stays locked. His litter box is upstairs, he's got water upstairs— there's no need for him to leave. So he stays, even if it's against his will.

Until recently, that is.

Before we left for France, Norton could not solve the system of the two locks. Soon after we got back, however, he did something that even I found a little scary.

We had guests one night, so the door was locked. Somewhere around two in the morning, I heard a scratching noise. I tried my best to ignore it, but after a minute or two that proved impossible, so I leaned over the bed to see what the hell was going on.

What was going on was that Norton was trying to lift the latch on the floor with his paw. I watched him claw at it once, twice, three times. Around the sixth or seventh time, he caught it and lifted it out of its notch. He then jumped straight up four or five times until he managed to swat at the waist-high hook that held both doors shut and unlatch that, too. With all the hard work done, Norton gently butted his head into one of the doors, swinging it wide open, then stepped nonchalantly out into the hallway and disappeared.

By this time, Janis was also wide awake and staring down at our little cat.

"You don't think . . ." she started to say to me.

"I *do* think," I told her, in a hushed tone.

We didn't have to say more than that. We were both remembering a moment in France. In the town of Sancerre, at a vineyard. It was the moment Norton saw that amazing dog stand on his hind legs, turn the doorknob, and open the door when he wanted to come in and out. That was the one thing in France that had seemed to overwhelm my cat. It was the only time he'd seen an animal do something he himself couldn't do.

"I don't believe it," Janis sputtered. "He couldn't still remember that. And even if he could, he couldn't make the connection . . . I mean, he just couldn't see that dog and . . . *Could he?*"

"Trust me," I said, nodding as her voice trailed off. "I know my cat."

about the author

Peter Gethers is a novelist, screenwriter, television writer, and publisher. In his spare time, he writes about his deeply sick relationship with his cat.